Unblinded Faith

Elisa Pulliam

HARVEST HOUSE PUBLISHERS
EUGENE, OREGON

Cover by JuiceBox Design

Cover design, illustration and hand-lettering: Kristi Smith—Juicebox Designs

Published in association with William K. Jensen Literary Agency, 119 Bampton Court, Eugene, Oregon 97404.

Unblinded Faith

Published by Harvest House Publishers
Eugene, Oregon 97408
www.harvesthousepublishers.com

ISBN 978-0-7369-7313-7 (pbk.)
ISBN 978-0-7369-7314-4 (eBook)

Library of Congress Cataloging-in-Publication Data

Names: Pulliam, Elisa, author.
Title: Unblinded Faith / Elisa Pulliam.
Description: Eugene, Oregon : Harvest House Publishers, 2018. | Includes bibliographical references and index.
Identifiers: LCCN 2018005339 (print) | LCCN 2017049636 (ebook) | ISBN 9780736973144 (ebook) | ISBN 9780736973137 (pbk. : alk. paper)
Subjects: LCSH: Faith. | Obedience—Religious aspects—Christianity.
Classification: LCC BV4637 (print) | LCC BV4637 .P85 2018 (ebook) | DDC 248.4—dc23
LC record available at https://lccn.loc.gov/2018005339

Printed in the United States of America

18 19 20 21 22 23 24 25 26 / BP-SK / 10 9 8 7 6 5 4 3 2 1

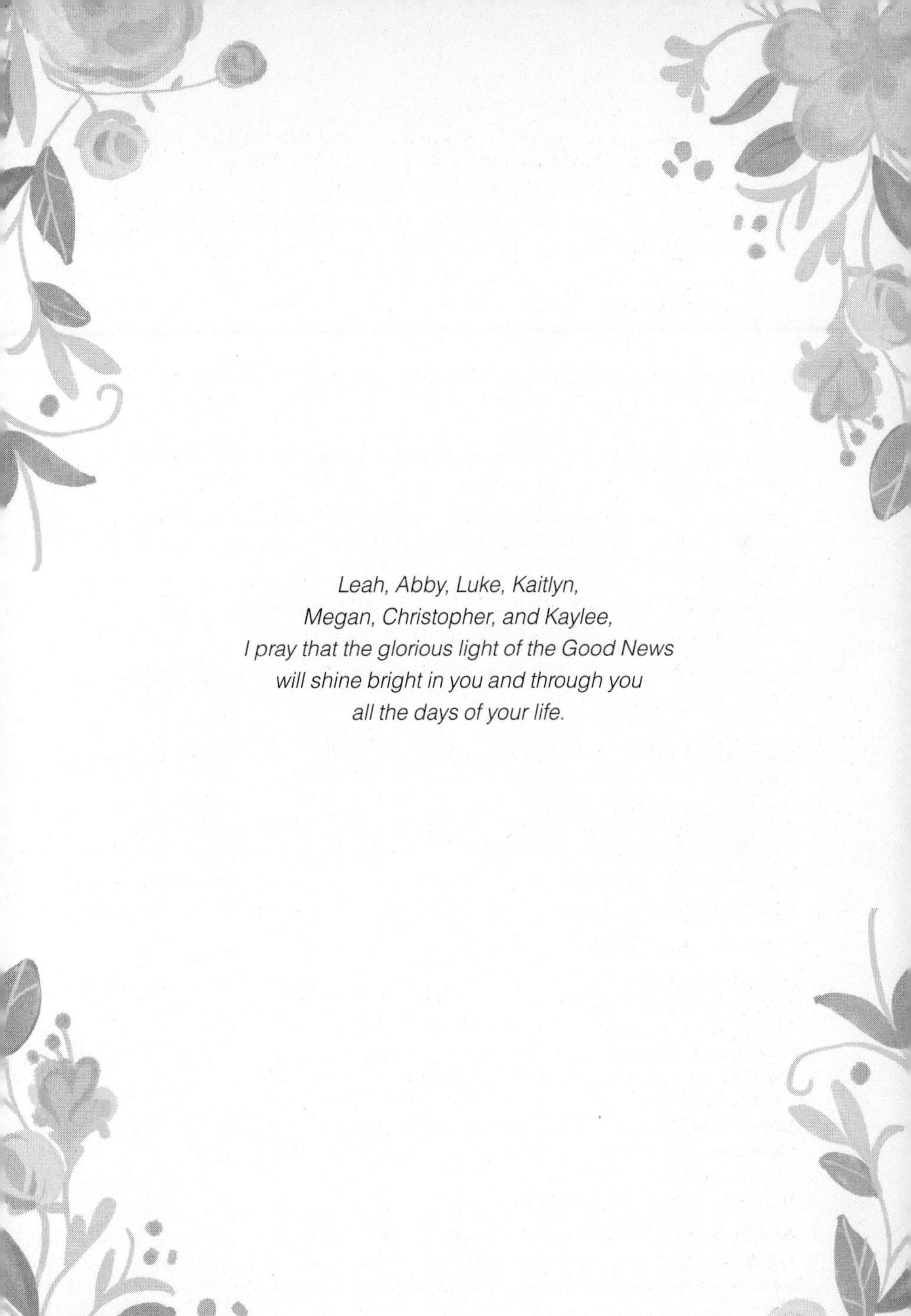

Leah, Abby, Luke, Kaitlyn,
Megan, Christopher, and Kaylee,
I pray that the glorious light of the Good News
will shine bright in you and through you
all the days of your life.

Contents

Foreword

I recently took the plunge and signed up for laser eye surgery to correct my terrible nearsightedness. After more than 20 years of wearing hard contact lenses, I was finally going to be free of their constraints and—after hearing multiple success stories—anticipated a new life of unobstructed vision. If you've had laser eye surgery, you know that there is a moment during the procedure (I'll spare you the details of what is actually happening in this brief moment) when you simply lose your ability to see. Your eyes aren't closed, there's nothing obstructing your view, and no eye drops are clouding your vision. Your vision simply goes static, like an old television set that has lost signal. In that moment, the vehicle for my sight was altered and unable to function properly until corrected. It happened quickly enough that fear couldn't set in, really, but for the first time in my life, I was truly aware of what a precious gift sight is.

We take for granted the ability to see in the same way we underestimate the gift of faith. We walk around, largely unaware that everything we take in from our surroundings and circumstances is directly affected by how well our eyes work…and in the case of spiritual sight, how clearly we see through our eyes of faith. If our eyes are the organ for sight, faith is the organ of perception for things unseen—for the trials you don't understand, the suffering you didn't anticipate, the change you don't grasp the purpose of. We cannot walk in the truth of God's love and redemption of our souls without exercising the muscle of belief and the organ of faith.

One of the ways we strengthen, exercise, and adjust the organ of faith is by aligning that faith with the truth from God's Word. Truth is how we measure whether we are walking according to our own wisdom or according to God's. Faith allows us to process and believe that truth so that it changes us.

Elisa Pulliam's heart beats for that change because faith changed her in ways she couldn't produce on her own. And so these explorations—these 90 short devotional readings—serve as an invitation to see better spiritually, see truer biblically, and see clearer the circumstances of our lives. The Word of God will actively correct the way we see all areas of our lives, and faith—unblinded faith—is the outcome of that exercise.

Friend, if your outlook spiritually has been static, fuzzy, or outright unclear, turn to the truth of God's Word and the guidance of Elisa's journey here. We were made to see.

~Ruth Chou Simons,
author of *GraceLaced*

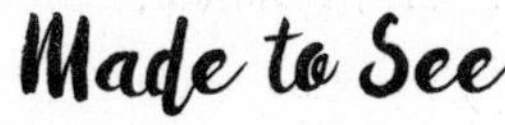

Made to See

Satan, who is the god of this world, has blinded the minds of those who don't believe. They are unable to see the glorious light of the Good News. They don't understand this message about the glory of Christ, who is the exact likeness of God.

2 CORINTHIANS 4:4

Are you ready to see by faith the very things of God that seem to elude you again and again?

Maybe you're like me. You want to believe the Bible is indeed true, but differing viewpoints, the noise of this world, and the trials of life make that hard. I get it, friend, if I may call you that already. Life is hard and confusing and filled with wandering and wondering about the goodness of God and promises found in His Word.

Doubt threatens to undo my faith at every turn. Does it also threaten yours? It's crazy how we can be certain of His extravagant grace and experience His sufficient power one minute and the next we're swimming in a sea of heartache and confusion. Do you feel this way too? At times I struggle to believe that God is who He says He is and I am indeed His beloved child. Can we choose to believe His Word as truth in spite of the circumstances that tempt us to question His sovereignty?

I once had a counselor say to me that I could write a book about every kind of issue imaginable, simply because of the proximity in which I've walked through situations with loved ones, friends, and even personally. Yes, that's why doubting God's goodness is my ongoing challenge, even though I can recount to you the amazing, miraculous ways I've witnessed His hand at work over the last twenty-plus years. You name it; I've been well acquainted with trouble of every kind.

I'm the child of divorce, have survived physical and emotional abuse, and endured family feuding and years of silence with loved ones. I continually battle the fear of breast cancer for my children and myself in light of our DNA. I've supported my closest friends through adultery, betrayal, and infertility. I've walked through cancer and brain tumors with dear friends (yes, plural), buried five suicide victims, experienced a community falling apart through a social media smear campaign, and coached countless women through hurt to healing as a result of division and betrayal in their ministry fields and churches. That's only half of it. But come to think of it, it sounds exactly like what God has already told us we'll be up against.

> *We are pressed on every side by troubles, but we are not crushed. We are perplexed, but not driven to despair. We are hunted down, but never abandoned by God. We get knocked down, but we are not destroyed.*
>
> 2 Corinthians 4:8-9

Trust me, some days I tell God I wish trouble would find someone else to hang out with, only to try to grab those words back because I wouldn't want another soul to endure half of what I've walked through. Even while my feelings may tell me otherwise, I know the truth deep in my soul that God is still our sovereign Lord, who has not removed His hand from our fallen world.

When trouble abounds, God is still on the throne.

I told that counselor I wasn't the least bit interested in writing such a book, because what good is a book about trouble? But I've since discovered that we need constant reminders to point us back to the promises of God—and a book about Scripture truths is a pretty good way to accomplish that mission. Because when we face the hardest parts of life, we need the Word of God manifested in Jesus Christ to be our steadying guide more than ever.

Maybe that's exactly what you need right now—maybe you're craving a stabilizing force in your life as the trials are breaking upon you like ocean waves before a storm. Maybe you're bewildered by the divine rerouting you've experienced and are searching for a hope-filled perspective so you can press forward. Or maybe your soul is satisfied and full, but you don't want to get complacent when it comes to steeping your life in God's Word.

No matter where you are in your journey of faith, I'm grateful that we get to walk through the next ninety days together. Because within these pages, God has a treasure in store for you through uncovering His promises with a resounding *yes* found in Jesus Christ.

> *All of God's promises have been fulfilled in Christ with a resounding "Yes!" And through Christ, our "Amen" (which means "Yes") ascends to God for his glory.*
>
> 2 Corinthians 1:20

Well, maybe our resounding yes sounds a little bit like *okay*. He'll take that, if it is all we have to give at the moment.

> No matter our story, no matter what is happening presently, and no matter what the future holds, God is who He says He is and will honor His promises to us until kingdom come.

The challenges we face daily will tempt us to despair, making it hard to trust that His ways are indeed perfect. We can't skirt around pain. We can't control the future. That's because we're up against the enemy of God, Satan himself. He is all about the business of blinding the minds of those who don't believe in the Good News while making the rest of us who do believe struggle to find clear vision in our faith (2 Corinthians 4:4).

But by faith we can make a choice about what we believe about God.

We can rest our mind on the sure foundation, the Word of God, in the same way the people of Corinth had to do in response to the apostle Paul's urging. Like us, the Corinthians doubted that God would be faithful and keep His word. But Paul reminds us, "Do you think I am like people of the world who say 'Yes' when they really mean 'No'?" (2 Corinthians 1:17). *Ahem.* How many people do you know who go back on their word? Maybe it's something you struggle with too. I know I do! But Paul points out plainly that Jesus is different.

When Jesus says yes, it is always *yes.*

With God, we don't need to read between the lines or interpret a hidden meaning. When He says His Word is true, it is always true. God's promises remain steadfast not only because of the work of Jesus Christ in our lives, but also through the manifestation of the Holy Spirit in our hearts—providing a guarantee for everything He has promised.

> *It is God who enables us, along with you, to stand firm for Christ. He has commissioned us, and he has identified us as his own by placing the Holy Spirit in our hearts as the first installment that guarantees everything he has promised us.*
>
> 2 Corinthians 1:21-22

Tell me: is there any human being who can make a guarantee like that? But isn't that the rub—we can't see God clearly because we judge Him from our earthly perspective when it should be the other way around.

We need to cultivate unblinded faith, which comes by believing God's Word is true.

God is not a magic genie we turn to only when we need a miracle. Nor is He a cosmic force in the sky, ready to zap us when we misbehave. God is our Maker, and inherent in His design is fellowship with His beloved. We are made in His image and crafted as a vessel to contain His Spirit. He longs to fill us with more of Himself, but we have to be willing. God won't force Himself upon us. We have a choice to embrace the fullness of God or to run hard and fast in the opposite direction. What will it be for you? Will you invite Him to infuse your heart, mind, and soul with more of Himself? Will you allow His Word to become your plumb line, rather than allowing your feelings to dominate your thought life?

Maybe you're afraid that choosing to believe God's Word as your source of truth will only make your journey harder. The reality is that a journey of faith is about as unpredictable as a drive through New York City heading for Long Island. Trust me, I know it well. But that doesn't make it better. You'll never know how long you'll be sitting in bumper-to-bumper traffic, with horns blaring incessantly, potholes large enough to swallow a MINI Cooper, and lights flashing from emergency vehicles responding to fender-bender accidents on roads without shoulders. Ah yes, chaos abounds. I think the same is true in our faith intertwined with real life.

Living with unblinded faith may feel a little uncomfortable at first, but it will bring about a kind of soul-filling hope found no other way.

How do I know? Because I spent the first 20 years of my life without faith in God or any knowledge of the truth as it is found in the Bible. During my junior year in college, God met me in a place where I was searching for meaning and purpose while running from the reality of my own brokenness. He captured my heart in a little dorm room in London with the promise of heaven and the hope of a fresh new start, making it easy to put my faith in Jesus Christ as my Savior. I make it sound as if it happened overnight, but God wooed me for years before I surrendered my life to Him. Maybe He's wooing you too...and inviting you to trust Him even more.

It took more than a decade of walking out my faith before I began reading the Word for myself. Honestly, the Bible overwhelmed me. I didn't know where to begin. Have you felt lost when it comes to reading Scripture too? Well, you're definitely not alone. But you don't need to stay in that place of feeling stuck.

The more you pursue God for understanding of His Word, the more He'll give it to you.

Actually, my very first attempt at reading Scripture began with a devotional similar to this one. It was placed in my hands by a friend the day after another friend told me that it was time to get serious about my faith. Ah, yes, divine appointments with good friends wholly submitted to the leading of God! That devotional provided the structure I needed for reading Scripture, as I juggled caring for little ones while working a part-time job. Let's just say I was short on time and lacking in emotional reserves. I didn't even try to make a morning quiet time happen. Instead, I set aside fifteen minutes at the beginning of my daughter's naptime to read the devotional.

I'm certain it was the Holy Spirit who led me to take the next steps to look up the Scripture references in context in my Bible, copy down a verse or two in my journal, and take a few minutes to pray by scribbling down my thoughts. I'm still using that same pattern for my devotional time with God, and it is one I hope will inspire you to embrace in this journey too. As a matter of fact, I recommend grabbing a journal so you can rewrite key Scripture principles and take a few extra minutes to jot down your thoughts about the reflection questions and prayer prompts at the end of each devotion. I promise that God will bring the Word alive in your heart as you soak it into your soul.

Reading the Word isn't about becoming more knowledgeable but rather being more equipped.

When Scripture is engrained in our minds and hearts, God uses it to sustain us through the ups and downs of life and fill us with an unquenchable hope, peace, and joy. Nothing else compares, because what we find in the Word is what we find in Jesus Christ, who is the Word (John 1). In the Word—in Jesus Himself—we find the way, the truth, and life we are after (John 14:6). Jesus promises us throughout Scripture that we will face trouble in this world (John 16:33). We will come up against opposition and feel completely out of place. This earth is not meant to be our forever home (Hebrews 13:14). We were made for eternity, but until we get there, we must live in this world and endure the trouble that is before us. So we must find our way through the muck and mire into hope-filled living by soaking in the truth and choosing to live it out (John 17:17). Through Christ and the Word, we will find our strength and a secure foundation on which to stand (Isaiah 33:6).

Unblinded faith cultivates unshakable hope.

Isn't that what you truly crave—not necessarily a faith that is an insurance policy against suffering, because that just doesn't exist, but rather a deeply rooted faith that is unwavering through the trials?

As I picture you holding this devotional in your hands, I'm asking God to reveal His truth to you in a fresh way and to give you a longing to know Him through Scriptures. My prayer is that you'll discover the true character of God and how to look for His presence in all your circumstances while also pinpointing the patterns and pitfalls to look out for in everyday life. Yes, God's instructions are as valuable as His promises to be faithful and kind, loving, and compassionate to you.

When you finish this journey, I don't want you to remember what you've read but rather whom you met—God Himself, manifested in your everyday life as your Lord and Savior, the Sovereign One, your Creator and Redeemer, Father and Friend, Provider and Rescuer, Holy Spirit and Counselor, and ultimate Guide.

May God inspire you to begin every day with unblinded faith as you make the decision to believe His Word as truth.

Journeying with you,

Lisa Pulliam

P.S. Before you get started, head over to http://www.unblindedfaith.com/to grab a free companion journal and other goodies.

1

Prepared and Equipped

All Scripture is inspired by God and is useful to teach us what is true and to make us realize what is wrong in our lives. It corrects us when we are wrong and teaches us to do what is right. God uses it to prepare and equip his people to do every good work.

2 TIMOTHY 3:16-17

Would you love to be prepared and equipped for the opportunities and even obstacles that come your way? How about being inspired by God in a way that makes you feel as if you have soul fuel to press on? Sounds good to me! But maybe that's because I'm kind of a preparation junkie. I wonder if that's an inherited trait... My mom is queen of preparations. Case in point: she must have thought I was going to Outer Mongolia with the way she packed for my freshman year in college. We filled a storage trunk with stockpiles of toiletries and cleaning supplies. A decade after graduating from college, I was still hauling around items from that trunk, which my husband teasingly referred to it as the traveling pharmacy.

We might laugh about it now, but the reality is, I'm also bent toward being overly prepared. I'll buy two of a grocery item, "just in case we run out." I'll have snacks in every bag, "just in case I get hungry." Can you relate? Yet I've lived long enough to know that being prepared with a storehouse of stuff doesn't compare to having a heart and mind prepared and equipped by God through His Word.

If we long to face each day prepared and equipped, we need to start each day inspired and steeped in the Word.

Within the Scriptures, we find all that we need for discerning what to believe as truth and what to do with the lies the Enemy of God will toss our way (John 3:16; 8:44; 14:6). Through reading the Word, we'll discover what to do with our sin because we can't handle it ourselves. That's the work of the cross, where Jesus laid down His life for our sin. We'll also learn how to experience the fullness of Christ dwelling in our hearts, infusing our lives with His peace, presence, and unquenchable joy. And we'll uncover the wisdom of God and how to make choices that keep us within the bounty of His blessings.

The Word is really the one and only training manual we'll ever need for living the full and abundant life God offers us (John 10:10), in spite of the challenges and trials we'll face. So what's standing in the way of using it?

READ

2 Timothy 3:14–4:5

RESPOND

God, I choose to embrace Your Word as truth, so that You may use it to teach me, correct me, and guide me, as You prepare and equip me for every good work. Thank You for providing it for my benefit. Forgive me when I neglect spending time in Your Word. Please decrease my distractions and increase my desire so I may spend time daily reading Your Word. In Jesus' name, amen.

REFLECT

What are the top three mind-sets or physical obstacles that keep you from spending time in the Word? What can you practically do to overcome each one?

If you've not grabbed a journal yet for this journey, I encourage you to do so and prayerfully seek God as you write down your answers to these questions. God will do such an amazing work in you, friend, as you devote this extra time toward reflecting and responding to His leading.

2

You Know Everything

You observe my wanderings and my sleeping, my waking and my dreaming, and You know everything I do in more detail than even I know.

PSALM 139:3 THE VOICE

Have you ever thought about how God is continually observing your life—noticing your wanderings and sleeping, waking and dreaming? How would it change your relationship with Him to settle into the truth that He is always watching over you, whatever you do and wherever you go?

As I moved through the doorway of the restaurant, I turned to count heads only to find out that we were missing our precious little miss. That's because I was in such a hurry to meet my dad, I jumped out of the car and scurried down the cobblestone block without looking back, figuring all my chickadees would quickly follow suit. Somehow my girl got left behind! My heart raced in triple time. Where could she be? I only took my eyes off of her for a moment. I imagined her whisked off by some perpetrator. But instead of retracing my steps, I urged my husband, "Go, go, go find her!"

Minutes later, they walked in the door together, and I grabbed that little babe as if I'd never seen her before. Turns out that everyone jumped out of the car, closing the doors while she was stuck in the way back. By the time she could get to the front to get out, everyone was gone, so she decided to stay put until we came back for her. I always told the kids that if we ever got separated in a public place, to stay at the last place we were together. She listened well, apparently, and quite calmly at that. There were no drama tears, but a few giggles over how she passed her time…sitting in the front seat and partaking of some gum while playing on her iPod. She knew we were coming for her. She knew we wouldn't abandon her. And so she kept on living without a fuss in the world.

Imagine if we lived with that kind of certainty of God's love and faithfulness—because, unlike this mama, God never takes His eyes off of us. He sees us...all the time.

> He made us, He watches us, He knows us better than anyone else in this world.

If we really believed this truth, would we be like my little girl, content to carry on with unshakeable peace permeating our souls?

READ

Psalm 139:1-24

RESPOND

God, I believe You know my wanderings and sleeping, waking and dreaming. You know everything I do in more detail than even I know. Thank You for Your faithful pursuit of my heart and Your constant hand on my life. Forgive me when I doubt Your promises. Help me believe that what You say, You mean, and what You mean, You do. In Jesus' name, Amen.

REFLECT

How does believing that God observes everything you do and sees you all the time change the way you can trust Him with your life?

3

Something New

I am about to do something new. See, I have already begun! Do you not see it? I will make a pathway through the wilderness. I will create rivers in the dry wasteland.

ISAIAH 43:19

How do you feel about God doing something new in your life? Do you embrace it or resist it? I have a love-hate relationship with change, even if God orchestrates it. I welcome a fresh start, where I can prayerfully lay before the Lord my hopes and dreams while surrendering my plans to His purposes. But I hate change that moves me out of my comfort zone and into God's new plans.

When we face a change or fresh start, what feels new to us is old news to God. He is about the business of doing "that new thing" long before we see it coming. He lays down the stepping-stones. He carves out the pathways. He has a greater purpose in mind than we ever imagine. Yet how often do we run from God's plans, preferring to stay immersed in the "as is" rather than trusting Him with the new thing He is doing! Maybe that's why God is always doing a new thing in our lives—He's setting the stage for our faith to deepen as we depend upon Him in more significant ways.

A life without risk forsakes the opportunities for our faith to grow.

Sometimes that new thing will be a dramatic move, a change in a job, or a ministry opportunity. But other times, His work may require us saying yes to a new way of thinking or living as we move through *that* obstacle or surrender *that* dream to Him. Instead of relocating our physical bodies, sometimes God will set the stage to move our hearts and minds closer to Him as we embrace His purposes afresh.

READ

Isaiah 43:1-7, 14-28

RESPOND

God, I believe You are always about the business of doing something new as you make pathways in the wilderness and rivers in the wasteland. Thank You for being willing to do a new thing, even though I may resist the kind of change that requires me to walk in faith. God, help me always say yes to what You are seeking to accomplish in my life. In Jesus' name, amen.

REFLECT

How may God be prompting you to embrace the new thing He wants to accomplish in your life?

4

Take Heart

I have told you these things, so that in me you may have peace. In this world you will have trouble. But take heart! I have overcome the world.

JOHN 16:33 NIV

What is your perspective about trouble? Do you find that the promise of it rocks your world? Or can you cling to the peace God offers you, knowing that Jesus has come to overcome the world?

I'm that girl who faces trouble with questions, desperately wanting to know how we got here so we don't have to go through it again. Of course, I also want to ask, "Why, God?" But I've discovered that a more productive question is, "What, God?" A *why* question doesn't change our circumstances, while a *what* question can change what we do going forward: *Lord,* what *do You want to accomplish in me and through me so that You get the glory?*

Submitting to the *what* question is really about recognizing that trouble is a reality on this side of the fall, while remembering that we're not in our forever home (Hebrews 13:14).

Heaven is the final trouble-free destination for the beloved of God!

As Jesus promised, "Very truly I tell you, you will weep and mourn while the world rejoices. You will grieve, but your grief will turn to joy. A woman giving birth to a child has pain because her time has come; but when her baby is born she forgets the anguish because of her joy that a child is born into the world. So with you: Now is your time of grief, but I will see you again and you will rejoice, and no one will take away your joy" (John 16:20-22 NIV). There is sorrow now, but the joy is coming when we see Him again.

So rather than expecting this life to be trouble free, we can embrace a new set of marching orders from God when we pursue Him with the *what* question and choose to walk out our days on this earth without despair.

READ

John 16:1-33

RESPOND

God, I know I will have trouble in this word, but I will take heart, because I believe Jesus has come to overcome the world. Even in trouble, I'm not beyond Your reach. Please give me eyes to see You at work, so that I may trust in You, watching for Your overcoming power to manifest in any and every situation. In Jesus' name, amen.

REFLECT

What trouble have you faced in your lifetime where you've witnessed the power of God overcoming on your behalf?

5

He Will Continue

I am certain that God, who began the good work within you, will continue his work until it is finally finished on the day when Christ Jesus returns.

PHILIPPIANS 1:6

Does the promise that God is still at work give you hope for what is yet to come? Maybe it's a promise you need to cling to for yourself or for someone you love.

During the summer before my sophomore year in college, I was invited to attend a youth event at a local church. I walked in with shaking knees and butterflies in my stomach, having never set foot in a church other than the one I grew up in. The worship music felt more like a rock concert, as opposed to the familiar acoustic rendition of "Here I Am, Lord," and the preaching seemed casual but personal.

The pastor shared about Jesus in a way I never heard before, explaining our need for a Savior to cover the debt of our sin. Honestly, I was a bit relieved, because I thought "being good" was the only ticket to heaven, and I was pretty sure that I was a shutout. Hearing the opposite was indeed good news, and the promise of heaven lured me to the altar to place my faith in Jesus Christ as my Lord and Savior. My friends circled around me, and after the tears stopped streaming down my face, someone in the group declared we should go for ice cream as a way to welcome me to the family. Who knew ice cream was a way to celebrate such a moment!

I returned home that night eager to relay the news to my parents, but they didn't share in my friend's enthusiasm. By morning, I heeded the parental advice to "forget about it" and move on...into the darkest and most destructive season of my life. But in His grace, God did not leave me or abandon me.

Sometimes what appears to be the end of the story is simply the end of a chapter.

God wasn't yet done with the work He began in me. He's not done with you either. Or your loved ones. The Lord is always at work, even when we don't see what He is doing, because He promises us that when He begins a good work in us, He will bring it to completion.

READ

Philippians 1:3-11

RESPOND

God, I believe that You, who began a good work in me, will bring it to completion. Thank You for being faithful to finish what You start, not ending until the day of Christ Jesus. Forgive me when I doubt Your work and Your Word. Give me vision to see all that You are doing, as I embrace Your purposes for my life. Give me patience to wait on You as You accomplish a work in those I dearly love. In Jesus' name, amen.

REFLECT

How have you presumed that God was finished with you, or a loved one? What if you believed that God were still at work, with full intentions to complete the good work He has begun?

6

Filled Souls

Father,out of Your honorable and glorious riches, strengthen Your people. Fill their souls with the power of Your Spirit so that through faith the Anointed One will reside in their hearts.

EPHESIANS 3:16-17 THE VOICE

What do you think it looks like for Jesus, the Anointed One, to reside in your heart?

Is something else crowding Him out? Could it be that unforgiveness has grown a root of bitterness in your heart? Or that jealousy has taken over? Maybe a fear or worry or an anxious thought has stolen square footage from Jesus.

What would it look like for Jesus to take back what belongs to Him—the space in your heart where He longs to dwell fully?

That's the question I find myself considering as I look at my closet. I know, it's strange. But see, I'd love to have a walk-in closet, yet as long as we're in our current house, I'll have to make do with the one I have. On the upside, I have to be choosy about the clothing I hang on to, because there's not a whole lot of room in my closet. As soon as my bedroom chair starts looking like a laundry basket, I know it's time to purge.

We can't hang on to everything without ending up with a mess spilling over. Likewise, as long as we're storing up junk in our emotional trunk, we're crowding out Jesus. We're also forgoing the strength and power God promises to us when Jesus Christ takes up full residence in our hearts.

Can you imagine inviting Jesus into your life in such a way that you give Him permission to roam freely throughout, settling into every nook and cranny while asking Him to kick those freeloading, no-good, life-draining residents to the curb? Why not ask Him to stay awhile and make Himself comfortable in your precious inner chamber—your heart?

READ

Ephesians 3:10-21

RESPOND

God, I receive Your glorious riches and strengthening so that You may fill my soul with the power of the Holy Spirit through Jesus Christ residing in my heart. Father, give me clarity and conviction on what is taking up space in my heart instead of You. Give me the desire to tackle those freeloading residents by Your power and strength, so there is more room for Jesus to dwell fully in my heart. In Jesus' name, amen.

REFLECT

Is it time for you to give Jesus permission to dwell fully in your heart, so that God's honorable and glorious strength and power may be in you?

7

Declare and Believe

If you openly declare that Jesus is Lord and believe in your heart that God raised him from the dead, you will be saved. For it is by believing in your heart that you are made right with God, and it is by openly declaring your faith that you are saved.

ROMANS 10:9-10

How do you think you can be made right with God? Could it really be as simple as openly declaring Jesus is Lord and believing in your heart that God raised Him from the dead that you may be saved by faith?

In those years that followed that youth service, when I gave my heart to the Lord only to deny Him before the breaking of dawn, I was desperately looking for unconditional love, not realizing that God already offered it to me. I thought I'd find the love I craved in Mr. Blue Eyes, but instead God used him to deliver it straight into my hands through His Word—literally.

Mr. Blue Eyes (aka the man who eventually became my husband) sent me a Bible with highlighted passages and a long letter in an effort to console me over the news of our friend's mom dying of cancer. I sat there, in my London dorm room, utterly confused by the package. How could the scriptures he pointed to make this situation any better or lighten the grief I felt? And so, I went to the one person I thought would have the answers. Susie was a pastor's daughter, clearly committed to living a Christian life. She talked about the Word as if it were alive. I brought her the letter, the Bible, and my questions. But instead of giving me an answer, she posed a life-changing question: "How do you think you're getting into heaven?" Yep, there was that question again—one I had turned from so brazenly. After all that had transpired since that youth night, I felt more disqualified than ever!

Do you feel you've lost your chance on God's love? That the promise of heaven is not for you? Well, friend, the good news is that God's love and acceptance isn't based on our past performance or current efforts.

Our goodness will never get us into heaven
because God's economy doesn't work that way.

When God sent His Son, Jesus Christ, to this earth to die for our sins, He did so because He loves us and knew we needed a Savior. He made it possible to be forgiven and receive the promise of eternity by declaring with our mouths that Jesus died on the cross for the forgiveness of our sins and believing in our hearts that He was raised from the dead.

Jesus is for those who know they need a Savior, and heaven is the promise for those who believe in Him as Lord. Forget the track record. Forget being ready. Forget the guilt and shame. Forget all the striving. And simply believe.

READ

Romans 10:5-13

RESPOND

God, I declare that Jesus is Lord and believe in my heart that You raised Him from the dead, so that I could be saved. I believe in my heart that Jesus Christ died on the cross for the forgiveness of my sins. Thank You for this gift of faith and for the promise of heaven as I surrender my life to You. God, show me who I can now share this good news with. In Jesus' name, amen.

REFLECT

How have you overcomplicated God's plan of salvation instead of simply heeding the call to confess with your mouth and believe in your heart that Jesus is Lord?

8

To Be Holy

They were calling to one another: "Holy, holy, holy is the Lord Almighty; the whole earth is full of his glory."

ISAIAH 6:3 NIV

Did you know that the only attribute of God described three times in a row in Scripture is in regard to God's holiness? *Holy, holy, holy*. There is no single other description of God that is emphasized like that.

The Hebrew word for *holy* is "qadowsh," which means, "sacred, set apart."[1] Wouldn't you say this describes God perfectly? He is unlike any human being we know. He is the creator of the world, the Sovereign One, and our heavenly Father. We may also know Him to be kind, merciful, gentle, tender, fierce, strong, compassionate, loving, and long-suffering as well, but these attributes pour forth from His inherent holiness.

The Trinity—the Father, Son, and Holy Spirit—proclaim the fullness of God's holiness. When the angel Gabriel announced to Mary that she would give birth to the Savior of the world, he said the child would be called "holy one" and that she would become pregnant by the power of the Holy Spirit (Luke 1:35 NIV). And when we place our faith in Jesus our Lord and Savior, believing that He died on the cross for the forgiveness of our sins, we receive the gift of the Holy Spirit and the presence of Christ dwelling in our hearts (Ephesians 1:4; 2:18; 4:24).

Our Holy God extends to us His holiness through faith in the Holy One, Jesus Christ.

How does that change the way you see God and yourself in light of this truth? Maybe you'll find you want to cry out in praise and sing,

"Holy, holy, holy is the Lord God Almighty, the whole world is indeed full of His glory"!

READ

Isaiah 6:1-13

RESPOND

God, I believe You are holy, holy, holy, and that the whole earth is full of Your glory. God, may I live in such a way that demonstrates my belief in You as set apart, awesome, and sacred, because of Your holiness. Fill me with the fullness of Your presence and cause me to yield to the leading of the Holy Spirit within me, that I may be part of Your purposes in filling this earth with Your glory. In Jesus' name, amen.

REFLECT

How does the holiness of God influence the way you see Him as well as yourself?

9

Let the Message Dwell

Let the message of Christ dwell among you richly as you teach and admonish one another with all wisdom through psalms, hymns, and songs from the Spirit, singing to God with gratitude in your hearts.

COLOSSIANS 3:16 NIV

What would it look like to have the message of Christ dwell richly in all your relationships? Can you imagine if it was really part of your norm to teach and admonish those you care about with wisdom from the psalms, hymns, and songs from God Himself, with gratitude in your heart? Can you imagine what it's like to be on the receiving end of that kind of conversation?

I've tasted this kind of Scripture-steeped relationship through the friendships forged while living and working at a Christian boarding school. It was a totally countercultural life in which the message of Christ dwelled richly among us, simply because of our routines. We shared meals in the dining hall, which commenced with saying grace or singing the doxology together. We gathered for daily chapel and Sunday worship, where we experienced biblical teaching and sang our hearts out together. We met for prayer as a way to engage in fellowship and rally around a crisis or need.

I know it was a privilege to be immersed in a Christ-centered community saturated in the truth of God. And I also know it's so much harder outside of that kind of setting! I've had to search for soul sisters since we moved, and I praise the Lord I've found them. So can you!

When Paul urged the Colossians to embrace the kind of relationships in which Scripture was ever present in an organic way, he did so because he knew that living in obedience to the Word requires honesty and holiness-focused accountability.

We're not meant to do this faith walk alone. We need "soul sisters" to lead us back to the heart of God and His Word.

Finding these kinds of friendships in which we can safely speak, teach, and admonish one another in psalms, hymns, and songs in the Spirit requires a sacrifice of time and intentional effort. Yet we're not in this pursuit alone. We can ask God to make accessible to us the kind of women who want to share a deep friendship with us, and in the meantime prepare ourselves by being steeped in the Word.

READ

Colossians 3:1-17

RESPOND

God, I choose to have the message of Christ dwell richly in me so I may teach and admonish with all wisdom through psalms, hymns, and songs from the Spirit with gratitude in my heart. Fill me with the message of Christ. May psalms, hymns, and spiritual songs overflow from my soul and out of my mouth at all times. Please bring into my life the kind of friendships in which this depth of faith is cultivated. In Jesus' name, amen.

REFLECT

How would you feel a deeper sense of Christ dwelling in you if psalms, hymns, and spiritual songs flowed out of you?

Head on over to http://www.unblindedfaith.com/soul-sisters/ to get access to a collection of downloadable resources, including a set of printable Scripture notecards, to send to your friends.

10

Soaring High

Those who trust in the LORD will find new strength. They will soar high on wings like eagles. They will run and not grow weary. They will walk and not faint.

ISAIAH 40:31

What do you think it means that by trusting in the Lord, we'll find new strength? Can you even imagine what it must be like to soar high on wings like eagles, run and not grow weary, walk and not faint?

I was young in my faith when I heard someone say, "God promises we'll soar on wings like eagles, but He didn't say how far off the ground we'll fly." I wonder, was that person speaking from a place of hurt or disappointment with God? Did she doubt God's ability? And did she realize her influence over me as she conveyed the smallness of God? I so clearly remember thinking, *Maybe I shouldn't expect so much from God.*

Maybe we make God small because we don't understand who He really is. Or maybe we doubt His promises because there is no way to get our earthly minds around what He offers us—like finding the strength we need through trusting Him more.

God is who He says He is, and He will always remain true to His Word.

It never crossed my mind to look up the verse in context of Scripture and discover for myself what God meant. If I had done so, I would have picked up two very important pieces of information. To begin with, the often-quoted verse comes at the very end of a chapter written by the prophet Isaiah declaring that God has no equal and He can do things the human mind can't even conceive. Isaiah unpacks the character of God, building toward the promise that we will find our strength by trusting in God. And second, the promise specifically says that we will fly "high" on wings like eagles—not low, not just above the ground, but high and soaring in the sky.

READ

Isaiah 40:12-31

RESPOND

God, I believe that by trusting in You I will find my strength, and that by Your power, You can make me soar high on wings like eagles, run and not grow weary, walk and not faint. Forgive me when I put my trust in anyone or anything but You and try to function on my own strength. Increase my dependence on You, so that I may gain the strength You provide. In Jesus' name, amen.

REFLECT

What portions of Scripture have you dismissed or misunderstood because they were misquoted or taken out of context? What steps will you take in the future to be more thoughtful about how you respond to biblical quotes and promises?

11

Perfect and True

God's way is perfect. All the LORD's promises prove true.
He is a shield for all who look to him for protection.

PSALM 18:30

Do you believe God's ways are perfect? Do you believe His promises are true? That He is a shield for all who look to Him for protection?

I wonder if it is hard to believe the truth about who God says He is in light of the digitally connected world we live in. Five minutes spent scrolling through my social media feed tells a story that's hard to digest, as one person after another requests prayer for a life-threatening health diagnosis, traumatic accident, or some sort of crisis. Five minutes spent reading the news points to world conflict, murders, missing people, and financial mishandlings. It's enough to make me wonder if God has completely turned His back on us. Do you feel this way too?

What we see and hear in this digital age is much more than our heart and, sometimes, faith can handle. Think about what life was like before social media and access to every news source. We would only know about what was happening in the lives of a handful of people—and those people would be ones we did daily life with in our families, churches, schools, and workplaces. Within those relationships, we would know the deep struggles but also the details of God's provision.

When our lives are sewn together in real life, we get access to the backstory, present story, and redeemed story—and we see evidence of God's faithfulness and provision.

So maybe the best thing to do is hone in on what God is doing right in front of us in the lives of those He's intended us to be intimately connected to daily. By pulling back from the social connections that simply drain our souls and cause us to doubt God's promises are true, we gain emotional and physical margin space to see and respond to the opportunities right in front of us. Maybe that looks like fixing a meal to bring to a family from church while they try to find their new normal after a crisis, or writing an old-fashioned note to a friend walking through a tough time.

When we embrace the opportunities to be fully present in the lives of those who need our physical touch, we also get front row seats to seeing God's power and provision at work.

READ

Psalm 18:25-36

RESPOND

God, I believe Your ways are perfect, You keep Your promises, and You are my shield when I look to You for protection. Help me in my unbelief. Show me how to guard my heart and mind from that which causes doubt. Reveal to me the perfect ways You go about fulfilling Your promises and protecting me. And show me how to step into the lives of those who need me to be Your hands and feet and mouthpiece. In Jesus' name, amen.

REFLECT

How have you witnessed God's faithfulness to His word, promises, and provision in the last three months?

12

The Promised Helper

I will ask the Father to send you another Helper, the Spirit of truth, who will remain constantly with you.

JOHN 14:16 THE VOICE

Is it hard for you to wrap your mind around the fact God has sent you a helper? Do you believe the Holy Spirit is really able to fill you with all truth and remain constantly with you?

The most profound, life-changing principles in Scripture are often the hardest ones to understand.

If only we had childlike faith! When my twins were still toddlers, I told them they needed to go bed at night to give all the workers in their body time to do their jobs—like growing them strong and healing their boo boos. I suspect they imagined Bob the Builder and his crew marching through their bodies. They didn't need a complex, scientific explanation of how sleep allows their human growth hormone to do its work to grow and repair their muscles and bones at a faster rate than when they are awake. Or that a lack of sleep reduces their white blood cell counts and the body's ability to fight off infection.[2]

When it comes to the working of the Holy Spirit and His part in the Trinity, a complex explanation doesn't necessarily lead to understanding. It's by faith that we experience the fullness of God at work in our lives; we choose to believe what we can't get our mind around. If Jesus asked His Father to send us a Helper, the Spirit of truth, who will be with us and always give us access to the truth, it's a matter of faith if we'll take Him at His word.

READ

John 14:15-31

RESPOND

God, I believe You have sent me a Helper, the Spirit of truth, to remain constantly with me. Thank You for giving me the Holy Spirit as my counselor to guide me in all truth. Although I may not understand Your ways, I pray You would increase my faith. In Jesus' name, amen.

REFLECT

What keeps you from believing God's promises, specifically that you have access to the Holy Spirit as your counselor, guide, and advocate?

13

A Quiet Life

Make it your goal to live a quiet life, minding your own business and working with your hands, just as we instructed you before.

1 THESSALONIANS 4:11

Have you ever considered the goals God has for the way we ought to live our lives? Maybe it takes you by surprise that one of those goals is to lead a quiet life, minding your own business and working with your hands.

I can't help but think of this particular verse in light of the technological world we live in today. Where's the quiet? It's filled with constant noise! How about the matter of minding your own business? Isn't reality TV and the invention of social media the exact opposite of that? Being a busybody is our form of entertainment. And it actually distracts us from the use of our hands, other than swiping across a screen a thousand times a day.

God has work for our hands to do. The question is whether we will join Him in it.

If we are really serious about heeding the call to live a quiet life, minding our own business, and working with our hands, we're going to have to risk being countercultural. Sure, we could take the approach of getting off social media, but I've seen good come from staying connected with friends around the country. So for me, the application of this verse looks like setting healthy boundaries regarding my usage. It also looks like being honest before God as I consider my habits, especially in light of the principles drawn from this passage in 1 Thessalonians 4: Am I living in a way that pleases God (verse 1)? Am I being holy, staying away from all sexual sin (verse 3)? Am I actively loving other believers (verses 9-10)?

An honest evaluation can motivate us to think more purposefully about how we're using our time for the glory of God. When we choose to live in a way that pleases God, seeking to be humble and holy, and to love deeply, we'll be positioned to fulfill the goal of living a quiet life, minding our own business, and working with our hands for the glory of God.

READ

1 Thessalonians 4:1-11

RESPOND

God, I will strive to lead a quiet life, minding my own business, and being busy with my hands, as You've instructed. Forgive me when I get caught up in everyone else's business. Forgive me when I get idle with how I'm using my time. Help me, Lord, to heed Your instructions as I seek to please You in the way I live. In Jesus' name, amen.

REFLECT

How can you make small changes that result in big impact in terms of leading a quiet life, minding your own business, and using your hands actively?

14

Unity in Community

May the God who gives endurance and encouragement give you the same attitude of mind toward each other that Christ Jesus had, so that with one mind and one voice you may glorify the God and Father of our Lord Jesus Christ.

ROMANS 15:5-6 NIV

What does biblical endurance and encouragement look like in the context of a community? And is unity in a community even possible?

> At the very point when we feel as if we can't do community any longer, we need to rely all the more on the Holy Spirit to manifest in us and through us, prompting us to take the next step forward.

As a life coach, I've heard more testimonies of broken communities than healthy ones. And I confess that's been my personal experience as well. How about you? I believe that's because the Enemy of God seeks to isolate us around our opinions and personalities as he strives to undermine the purposes of God. He knows that if we unify with the mind of Christ, God will get all the glory as He accomplishes His kingdom purposes.

What does that look like? Well, maybe it requires enduring another round of discussions emerging from differing opinions. Or approaching a conflict by slowing down to seek wisdom from the Word. Maybe it looks like engaging the disengaged and reaching out to the hurting.

Unity in community is about laying down our agendas, admitting our weaknesses, and leaning into the strength found among those God has ordained for us to be in relationship with. It really is a gift from

God that, if we're willing to receive it, will unfold a blessing while giving Him all the glory.

READ

Romans 15:1-7

RESPOND

God, I believe You will give me endurance and encouragement, so I may share the same mind-set and experience unity within other believers. Father, forgive me when I let my personal preferences get in the way of Your purposes. Forgive me when I hide my weaknesses instead of partaking of the strength offered in the family of God. Please use me to foster unity in community around Your purposes for Your glory. In Jesus' name, amen.

REFLECT

What does it look like to embrace the mind of Christ as you pursue unity in your community through the work of the Holy Spirit?

15

From Triggered to Trapped

We demolish arguments and every pretension that sets itself up against the knowledge of God,and we take captive every thought to make it obedient to Christ.

2 CORINTHIANS 10:5 NIV

Have you ever noticed how easily our emotions dominate our lives? We feel, therefore we are. *Au contraire.* We are, because we've not taken into account what we feel. Yes, feelings matter. They can't be avoided, because those raw emotions are brought on by a never-ending barrage of triggers.

We are susceptible to triggers through all our senses—sight, sound, smell, touch, and even taste. The color of the sky might bring to memory that awful Saturday afternoon when we heard the bad news. The smell of the spring air can trigger feelings from that last day together. A song playing in the background at the department store brings back the emotions you experienced when your heart broke for the first time.

Our senses will always elicit a reaction, but in Christ we can choose a response that lines up with the truth.

In life coaching, we call this being "response able," as we build into our routines the practice of gaining awareness about our triggers and taking strategic steps to choose our reaction wisely. The goal isn't to have a scripted response but rather to manage our emotions in light of the truth. Isn't that what Paul is urging us to do by taking captive every thought and making it obedient to Christ?

Friend, our minds are the battleground where the Enemy wages war on our life. We have to demolish the lies of the Enemy and not allow our feelings to spiral us into a pit of defeat (John 8:44). Only when our thought life is rooted in God's Word will His promises, principles, and commands become the guiding force of our lives.

READ

2 Corinthians 10:1-6

RESPOND

God, I will strive to take captive my thoughts and make them obey Christ, so that every proud obstacle that keeps me from knowing Jesus more fully will be destroyed. I know I cannot allow my emotions to dictate how I live. Give me the courage to demolish the lies that come my way and replace them with the truth, that I may live according to Your Word in every area of life. In Jesus' name, amen.

REFLECT

How can you begin the habit of trapping your thoughts to make them obedient to Christ, especially in light of your most common emotional triggers?

16

Transformed Living

Don't copy the behavior and customs of this world, but let God transform you into a new person by changing the way you think.

ROMANS 12:2

Do you feel there is a particular pattern informing the way you choose to live your life? In other words, what is shaping your thought life? Dictating your habits? Setting your routines into motion?

Our lives are predominately influenced by our family of origin and cultural upbringing. We're influenced by our heritage as well as the generational themes that form our values during the first twenty years of life. Can you see how this is true in your own life?

For me, the tension between what was once a normal part of my upbringing and the new expectations for how I ought to live as a follower of Christ required me to make a shift in my thinking and living. For example, I struggled in choosing to spend time with people over taking care of things. Clean bathrooms and organized cupboards trumped connecting heart-to-heart, until I realized God is more concerned with the heart than appearances and accomplishments (1 Samuel 16:7; Romans 12:10; Matthew 6:19-20). I also had to cope with the fact that the way I screamed and yelled when I was angry (over nothing worth getting that hyped up about) was indeed sin, as opposed to my right to express my feelings as my family of origin was accustomed to doing (Ephesians 4:26).

Our inherited beliefs form a pattern of thought that shapes the way we live—unless we allow God to challenge our thinking and thereby transform our living.

God was so kind to begin the process of challenging me through attending a Bible study at church. Ironically, the friend who invited me never actually showed up. I refer to that moment as a divine setup for me to step up in spiritual maturity! Although my motivation for attending was to snag a few hours each week with other adult women while my kiddos went to the childcare, God used that time to cultivate in me a hunger for the Word. I learned how to read Scripture and apply it—and applying it was the critically important part. That's how the pattern of my life changed, and the same can happen with you. When we soak up the Word and let it inform our thoughts, God moves us from our old ways of thinking and living into new mind-sets and actions that reflect the unadulterated, unopinionated, and totally raw Scriptures we've consumed for ourselves.

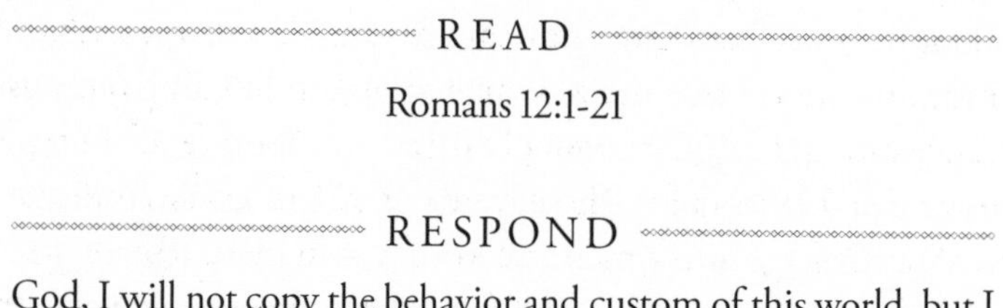

READ

Romans 12:1-21

RESPOND

God, I will not copy the behavior and custom of this world, but I will let You transform me into a new person by changing the way I think. Thank You that Your Word is my source of truth and that within Scripture I find the pattern for how to live my life. Thank You that You have the power to transform me from the inside out when I give You access to my thought life with a willingness to line up my thinking with Your Word. In Jesus' name, amen.

REFLECT

How are you making time for God to transform your life by allowing His Word to change the way you think?

17

Both / And

Notice how God is both kind and severe. He is severe toward those who disobeyed, but kind to you if you continue to trust in his kindness.

ROMANS 11:22

Do you believe God can be both kind and severe? Is that too much to get your heart and mind around?

An expression comes to mind when I read this verse: "It's both/and." I can hear my old boss use these words more than two decades ago to describe the way we went about fulfilling our mission at the boarding school. He would say we were "both/and" in terms of character and excellence. These were our pillars, essential in the process of training up young men and women to know and serve the Lord.

Wouldn't you agree that "both/and" is true in so many areas of our lives? In our work, we experience the "both/and" of fulfilling our tasks to the best of our abilities and still make room for relationships. In our families we have the "both/and" of loving sacrificially and being unconditionally loved. In stewardship of our bodies, we have the "both/and" of fitness and rest. But when it comes to God, we're not so crazy about the "both/and" because we only want the side of His character that makes us feel safe and comfortable, not accountable and convicted.

God's attributes may seem opposite in their nature, when they are actually necessary for balance.

God is and always will be "both/and," and that's actually the very thing we count on. Because of His love for us, God sent His one and only Son, Jesus, to lay down His life for our sin. Through Christ's death, we find our new life and the promise of eternity. Yes, God restrained

Himself when He could have punished us for our chronic state of disobedience and unintentional sin. Through Jesus submitting to His Father's will, He became a vessel of God's righteousness and humility, mercy and justice, grace and love. He didn't eradicate God's anger and wrath, but rather provided the counterpart, making our understanding of God's love all the more profound.

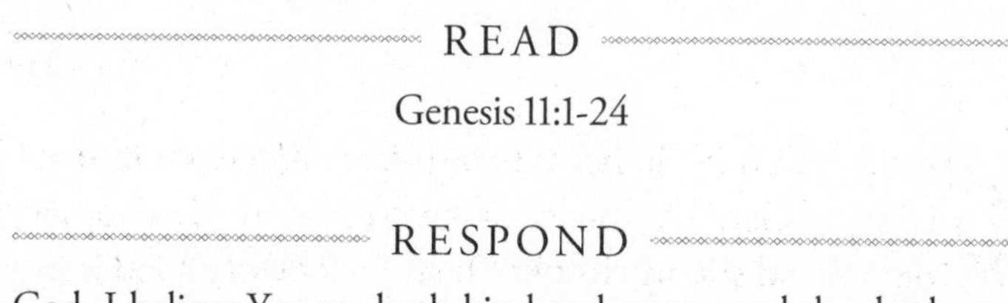

READ

Genesis 11:1-24

RESPOND

God, I believe You are both kind and severe, and that both are attributes of Your character that You will use for good. Please forgive me for the times I want to pick and choose Your attributes. Please mature me in my faith and understanding of Your character, so that I may wholeheartedly embrace Your whole truth. In Jesus' name, amen.

REFLECT

How have you ignored the fullness of God's attributes because you've wanted only the ones that make you feel good?

18

Be Still

Be still and know that I am God!

PSALM 46:10

What do you think it means to be still in order to know that God is indeed God? Do you feel as if you're supposed to stop all your "doing" and simply sit still? Or could it be that God is suggesting stillness in your heart and mind?

For years, the words of a dear family member urging me to "just sit still already" made me wonder if I had a problem or if she did. Of course I wanted to sit still and do nothing. But what about that laundry that needed folding? The dishes to be washed? The pile of bills to be paid? It's not that I can't or won't be still. Rather, my God-given observation abilities and overdeveloped sense of responsibility get in the way of finding calm in the middle of chaos. If I am to truly slow down, my space needs to be picked up and the basic to-do list tackled. Can you relate?

The way we embrace stillness before God will be entirely reflected in the way He uniquely made each one of us.

Being still isn't about chores or hobbies or work being put aside. Choosing to be still before God is about refusing to fuss when life spins out of control. God doesn't need us to figure it all out, because He's already got everything taken care of. It's about surrendering to God a solution we'd rather find out on our own.

Oh, yes, friend, when we slow down, it's not "to do" nothing—it's an opportunity to sit quietly with God and meditate on His Word, getting to know Him more intimately as we trust that He will take care of the details of life.

READ

Psalm 46:1-11

RESPOND

God, I will choose to be still, so I may truly know You more. Please enable me to trust You with everything that is left undone as I sit with You. Give me a desire for a deeper, more abiding relationship with You. Please instill in me an understanding of Your faithfulness through reading Your Word as I seek to know You more. In Jesus' name, amen.

REFLECT

How can you embrace the way God made you while making time to be still with Him each day?

19

Compassionate and Merciful

The Lord is compassionate and merciful, slow to get angry and filled with unfailing love.

PSALM 103:8 NIV

When you search the Scriptures, you find multiple places that describe God's character as compassionate and merciful, slow to get angry, and rich in unfailing love. And yet, would you agree that it is not always easy to believe that the Scriptures are preaching truth? Is that because the consequences of sin—your own or someone else's—make it feel as though God's compassion and mercy are far off? Do you feel as if His anger has been unleashed upon you alone? Is His unfailing love seemingly out of reach?

Probably the biggest challenge for me is to believe that our behavior is not at the center of God's focus. For far too long I thought that for God to show me His compassion, mercy, and love, I had to earn it. And trust me, that was never going to happen. What a relief to discover that God couldn't love me any more or any less than He already does. The same is true for you.

God's mercy isn't linked to a measuring stick. He's not some hot-tempered, irrational killjoy ready to ruin our lives with unquenchable anger.

God's love for us is not based on our performance, but it is reserved for those of us who have been adopted into His family through faith in Jesus Christ (Ephesians 1:4-5). He instructs us, His children, to show Him reverence and seek to love Him with all our being as He chooses to keep His covenant and remembers His promises from everlasting to everlasting (Psalm 103:17-18; Deuteronomy 6:5). God is always compassionate and merciful, not easily angered and unfailing in love. Because God is always who He says He is and will always do what He says He will do.

READ

Psalm 103:1-22

RESPOND

God, I believe You are compassionate and merciful, slow to get angry and filled with unfailing love. Thank You that You are who You say You are. Please forgive me for the times I've doubted Your character. Help me see You through the lens of truth, striving to love You with all my being and fearing You alone. In Jesus' name, amen.

REFLECT

In what ways have you witnessed the compassion, mercy, patience, and unfailing love of God in your life in the last week, month, year, and maybe even lifetime?

20

Stone to Flesh

I will give you a new heart and put a new spirit in you; I will remove from you your heart of stone and give you a heart of flesh.

EZEKIEL 36:26 NIV

What would you say is the state of your heart? Is it hardened, maybe from the disappointments and devastation you've experienced in your past? Is it soft, full of God's love overflowing through you?

My heart has been both. It was hard until the Lord transformed the stony places to flesh. The process took me by surprise, as He drew me into the book of Ezekiel, written by a priest who was called by God to prophesy destruction over Israel for their rebellion. Happy times, I tell ya! Fortunately, I had no idea what I was getting into when I heeded the Holy Spirit's leading to crack open my Bible, grab a journal, and start studying. I pored through one chapter after another, completely bewildered and utterly confused by Ezekiel's prophecies—except for one verse.

In Ezekiel 36:26, the prophet describes how God takes a stony, stubborn heart and turns it to tender, loving flesh—that promise felt so incredibly personal as I considered the matter of stubbornness and the weight of stones residing in my own heart. Over the next year, I often asked God what to do about those stones, and through the help of a godly counselor, He gave me the courage to go in for the dig. One memory at a time, He pulled back each layer of sediment, formed by stones of guilt, shame, bitterness, and anger. As He unpacked those stones—those wounds—He made room in my heart for Jesus to dwell more fully.

The Lord can turn our stony hearts into His dwelling place, transforming us with one healing truth at a time.

Even if you don't have a backstory like mine, marred by abuse and rebellion, is it possible that you've allowed offenses and disappointments to harden your heart? Friend, I pray you'll join me in the daily process of giving God access to our hearts, so only He may take up residence in us and flow through us onto those we love.

READ

Ezekiel 36:16-38

RESPOND

God, I want You to turn my stony heart into a heart of flesh. Give me the courage to approach You with confidence, trusting You with all I've stored up in my heart. Heal my wounds and fill me with more of Jesus, that Your love, grace, and forgiveness would fill my heart to overflowing. In Jesus' name, amen.

REFLECT

How is God prompting you to give Him your heart so He can transform the hardened parts to flesh?

Head on over to http://www.unblindedfaith.com/study/ for a selection of simple but effective Bible studies that will help you become a student of the Word and yield your heart to God more fully.

21

Freed by the Truth

Jesus said to the people who believed in him, "You are truly my disciples if you remain faithful to my teachings. And you will know the truth, and the truth will set you free."

JOHN 8:31-32

Would you say you have experienced the kind of spiritual and emotional freedom that comes from being faithful to God's teachings and believing His Word? Or is there something in your heart and mind that keeps you from believing the truth and the freedom it offers?

It's kind of hard to get our minds around this particular promise, don't you think? How can freedom come through faith? What about the reality of life we live in? Is this freedom only in regards to what happens in the spiritual realm?

Freedom in Christ is a soul-deep, unshakable, unquenchable gift that manifests in every single breath drawn from believing the truth.

It's not a freedom from responsibility or accountability. We don't get a free pass from obstacles or challenges. Nor do we get to avoid trials or temptations. We absolutely endure the reality of life on this earth. What Jesus is talking about is the kind of freedom that comes through no longer being slaves to sin that leads to death.

In obedience to the Father, Jesus came to set us truly free—free to experience life in which sin doesn't hold us captive. He has already defeated sin and death on our behalf. But will we accept what He has done? Will we remain faithful to the teachings found in Scripture? Will we believe that Jesus is indeed our Redeemer, making a way to be with God in heaven through eternity?

READ

Matthew 8:21-36

RESPOND

God, I will remain faithful to Jesus' teaching, so I may experience a life set free by truth. Thank You, Jesus, for Your obedience to the Father on my behalf. Thank You for setting me free from sin that leads to death. May I make much of Your sacrifice by remaining faithful to You and the Word. In Jesus' name, amen.

REFLECT

How is God prompting you to remain faithful to His teachings and believe more fully in the power of Jesus Christ to set you free from sin that leads to death?

22

Root and Fruit

The seeds on the rocky soil represent those who hear the message and receive it with joy. But since they don't have deep roots, they believe for a while, then they fall away when they face temptation.

LUKE 8:13

What do you think it means for love to be the soil where life takes root? If you've got a green thumb and don't mind getting your hands into the dirt, you probably already understand the metaphor. Personally, I have no desire to do what it takes to tend properly to an outside garden or even pay attention to the simple needs of my houseplants. I overwater my succulents and underwater the outside hanging baskets. I use whatever soil I can find, ignoring the rocks that will become root-growth barriers while forsaking the importance of fertilizer. I suppose I should give up trying to keep the darling plants alive and simply go for the best plastic imitations I can find. If only I didn't fall madly in love with the idea of it all and neglect to count the cost. Can you relate?

If we are fickle gardeners of our faith, lacking the perseverance to nurture the soil of our hearts, we'll not experience the spiritual growth we crave.

A lack of spiritual fruit in your life may actually be a root problem. So what's keeping those roots from growing down deep? Is it a matter of unrealistic expectations? Do you want your time in the Word to always feel good? Is it hard to get honest with God? Do you feel as if He might not answer your prayers? Are you simply neglecting time with God?

Maybe you get going on a Bible reading plan, only to find you lack the accountability and motivation to stay disciplined. Do you neglect your prayer time because you're disappointed by God's answers and don't want to be bothered turning over the soil of your heart again?

Yes, these are tough questions to answer, but tackling them is like pulling out the weeds and pinpointing the kind of nutrients the soil of your heart desperately needs.

READ

Luke 8:4-15

RESPOND

God, I want to receive Your message with joy but don't want to fall away when temptation comes because I don't have deep roots. Give me a desire to be in Your Word so I can grow roots down deep—the kind that will enable me to withstand the test of time and trials ahead. Please surround me with people who will remind me to tend my garden of faith and cultivate nutrient-rich soil in my heart. In Jesus' name, amen.

REFLECT

What habits could you develop that would help you grow deep roots of faith that will sustain you during temptation and trials?

23

No Trouble

See to it that no one falls short of the grace of God and that no bitter root grows up to cause trouble and defile many.

HEBREWS 12:15 NIV

May we continue on this gardening theme for a bit, as we consider how a deep root system influences the rest of our lives? After living through three horrific hurricanes, I've come to understand God's design for a root system as the stabilizing force not only through the storms of life, but also in between. That latter truth became abundantly clear when one of the most beautiful trees that once stood near our home came tumbling down on a sunny fall afternoon.

We knew that tree was dying from the way its leaves didn't quite hold on for the full season and the branches grew barer over time. But we had no idea how bad things were under the surface. Disease shriveled the roots to brittle nothingness. With the sopping wet ground from an unseasonably rainy fall, the tree didn't have deep enough roots to hold it upright on a windless fall afternoon. Isn't that interesting—the great oak tree withstood at least two hurricanes while we lived on that property, and endless snowstorms, but without a healthy root system it couldn't survive one more day of mild weather. Isn't that true about us?

We might endure for a season, but that doesn't mean our spiritual root system is healthy.

We can easily be like that tree, whose roots were destroyed by disease, even though the evidence appeared mild—until the day it fell. Sin can take root in our lives instead of God's Word. Hurt can make us vengeful as we refuse to forgive and trust God to be just and merciful. A bitter root can easily grow in our hearts, separating us from God and destroying our relationships, our testimonies, and everything good in our lives. Let us not neglect even one hint of spiritual disease, but tackle it and treat it by seeking God for every bit of healing.

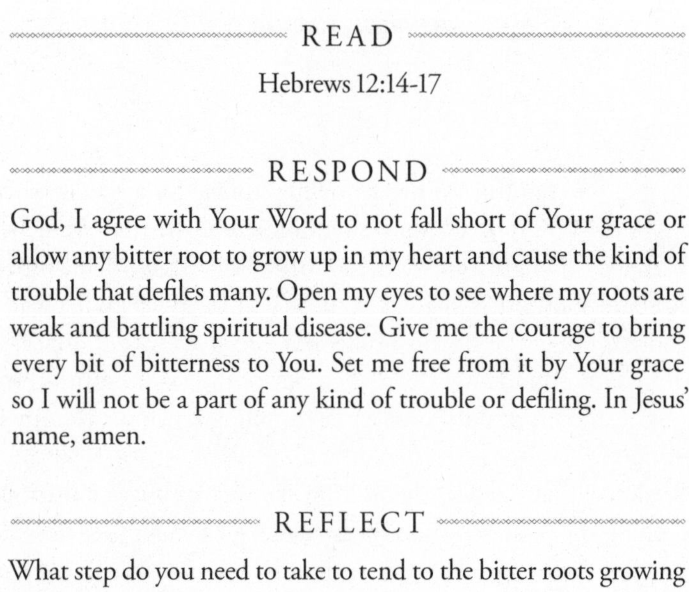

READ

Hebrews 12:14-17

RESPOND

God, I agree with Your Word to not fall short of Your grace or allow any bitter root to grow up in my heart and cause the kind of trouble that defiles many. Open my eyes to see where my roots are weak and battling spiritual disease. Give me the courage to bring every bit of bitterness to You. Set me free from it by Your grace so I will not be a part of any kind of trouble or defiling. In Jesus' name, amen.

REFLECT

What step do you need to take to tend to the bitter roots growing up in your heart?

24

Love Is the Goal

Let love be your highest goal!

1 CORINTHIANS 14:1

How would your life be different if love were your highest goal? When I think of my life goals, love has not been on the top of the list. Instead, I've focused on peace, which I am sure is a result of the chaos that marked my childhood. Love, well, I could take it or leave it. But when it comes to the state of my relationships and the temperament in my home, it's peace I'm after. And yet, if love were my highest goal, wouldn't peace follow along? You can't be hollering at each other and also declaring your love for one another. You can't ignore each other's practical needs and also live in peace together.

Love ushers in the kind of peace our hearts crave.

Maybe that's why Paul gave the instructions in 1 Corinthians 14 to "let love be your highest goal" right after finishing an entire chapter about what love looks like. It's as though he is saying, "Now that we've got that matter settled, start loving as if it were your only goal."

If we embrace the call to love well, long, deep, and wide, won't that change everything? Imagine how a deeply committed, God-overflowing love could influence all our relationships—with our family and our friends, those we work with and serve alongside, and even strangers who are hungry for the hope of Christ we can offer them through our love in action.

READ

1 Corinthians 13:1–14:1

RESPOND

God, I will make love my highest goal. Thank You that love was Your highest goal as You gave Your one and only Son, Jesus, to die on the cross on my behalf. May I receive Your gift of love and honor You by making love my highest goal as well. In Jesus' name, amen.

REFLECT

How is God moving you toward making love your highest goal?

25

Unchangeable

One day Jesus left the crowds to pray alone. Only his disciples were with him, and he asked them, "Who do people say I am?" "Well," they replied, "some say John the Baptist, some say Elijah, and others say you are one of the other ancient prophets risen from the dead." Then he asked them, "But who do you say I am?" Peter replied, "You are the Messiah sent from God!"

LUKE 9:18-20

How would you answer this question Jesus posed to the disciples about who He really is? Would you say Jesus is God's Son? The Messiah? Or just a man who walked in sandaled feet a long time ago?

When I arrived home from that semester in London, I was fully bent on telling the world about Jesus. He became my Messiah, my Savior, and the Lord I was living for. I was so full of faith, overflowing with enthusiasm for the hope of the gospel. And yet, that hope was somehow not attractive enough to my family and friends for them to consider the claims of the Messiah for themselves. They humored me with comments like, "Oh, that's nice. Well, whatever works for you," and, "It's so good you found religion. I'm sure it will be a great crutch for you."

The gospel message doesn't change, regardless of what we choose to believe.

I figured in time, they'd come to see Jesus the way I did—they simply needed a chance to process it all. Well, time has passed. More than twenty-five years by the time you read these words, and I am still proclaiming Jesus is the Son of God, the Messiah, and the giver of all hope. I fully believe He lived a life we could not live and died a death we could not die. And I still want those I love the most to share this hope, power, grace, and truth I've found in Jesus Christ.

Jesus is and always will be the Messiah, the anointed and holy One sent by God. He is the Great I Am, Redeemer, and Great Rescuer, Friend and Savior to all who choose to call on His name and believe He is who He says He is.

READ

Luke 9:10-20

RESPOND

God, I believe Jesus was more than a man who walked this earth—He was and is the Messiah sent by You. God, give me the courage to never waver in my faith, shy away from my testimony, or run from sharing the good news for Your glory. In Jesus' name, amen.

REFLECT

How do you answer the question Jesus posed to Peter, "Who do you say I am?"

26

Redeemed for Good

You intended to harm me, but God intended it all for good. He brought me to this position so I could save the lives of many people.

GENESIS 50:20

Have you felt as if the Enemy of God has set out to harm you, but you're standing in a place where you can see how God intended it for good? Maybe you can see how God has brought you to a particular position in life to use what Satan hoped would destroy you for the saving of many lives.

As a life coach, I've been privy to stories of so many women experiencing real-life schemes of harm, just like Joseph experienced at the hands of his brothers. Yet despite living in a world plagued by sin, I've not lost hope that God's purposes will prevail for us as they did for Joseph. In the same way that "The Lord was with Joseph," God is still with us (Genesis 39:2) .

We may not be privy to God's redemptive work in our story, but that doesn't mean He's stopped accomplishing His purposes for His glory.

We can lean in to the truth of God's faithfulness as we think about how God moved Joseph into greater roles of influence until the moment when his story clearly displayed God's glory. While Satan intended harm, God intended to use Joseph's life in the saving of many lives. Is it possible that God is accomplishing that mission in your life right now, even if you don't see what He is doing?

There was a time in which Joseph wasn't clued into God's purposes. And yet, did he cooperate with God's plans? Joseph could have justifiably responded in anger and sought revenge, but instead he chose compassion and mercy on his brothers. Was that because he had already reconciled to God the twists and turns of his life? Maybe that's why I love Joseph so much—because he gives us a perspective on how to be a survivor submitted unto the Lord, believing that His plans for good will always prevail.

READ

Genesis 50:14-20

RESPOND

God, I believe that what was intended to harm me, You can intend for good, so that You may save many people. You are a God who rescues, redeems, and restores. Thank You for taking the plots of the Enemy and reworking them for good. Lord, help me trust in Your work. Prepare my heart for the day You will make Yourself known and open the doors to reconciliation. In Jesus' name, amen.

REFLECT

How do you see God at work in your story, using what was intended to harm for good and maybe even for saving many lives?

27

Our Hope

Let your unfailing love surround us, Lord,
for our hope is in you alone.

PSALM 33:22

What do you hope in? Or better yet, whom do you hope in? Is your hope found in God and His unfailing love? Is it found in the promises delivered through the cross? Or are you tempted to hope in your circumstances, people, and outcomes?

There was a time in my life when my hope came from the outcome of my efforts rather than in the Provider Himself. Like that time I hoped I'd win a writing contest and be rewarded with a free ticket to a big-name conference. After doing everything I could to position myself as a contender, and praying incessantly for God to give me favor, I was left to hope—as in waiting expectantly, wondering if God's will matched mine.

The truth was, my hope was not in the Lord's purposes. It was in my purposes, and I wanted God to bend His knee to them. And, well, He didn't. I didn't win that contest or any other for that matter. But maybe "failing to win" was God's plan to get me to the place of complete surrender as I laid my dreams at His feet.

When we put our hope in God Himself, we are actually placing everything about our lives in the arms of His love.

How often do you put your hope in a plan or person, worldly promise, or self-made provision? It's natural since we don't know the mind of God or how He'll choose to work in our lives. But this we do know: God's perfect plan is what we can put our hope in. He made us and He has a purpose for us that lines up with His greater kingdom plan that will bring Him all the glory (Psalm 33:15).

READ

Psalm 33:1-22

RESPOND

God, I believe Your unfailing love is with me, even as I put my hope in You. Please, Lord, increase my trust in Your character and faithfulness. Help me uncover the lies I believe about who You really are. May I walk in confidence before You, knowing You are never changing, always faithful, and completely worthy of my hope. In Jesus' name, amen.

REFLECT

What would it look like to put your hope in God alone as you trust in His unfailing love?

28

Good Gifts

"If you sinful people know how to give good gifts to your children, how much more will your heavenly Father give the Holy Spirit to those who ask him."

LUKE 11:13

Do you think of God as a good Father, who is about the business of giving His children good gifts? Or has your experience with your earthly dad made this perspective challenging? And when you think of good gifts, are you imagining something tangible, like a house or car, a job or a vacation?

My parents divorced shortly after I came to know the Lord and my relationship with my dad took a turn for the worst, culminating in a horrible falling out. I felt like an orphan on so many levels—a fatherless daughter. I couldn't understand how it could be God's will for me and questioned how He was about the business of giving good gifts, if He wouldn't even give me my dad back. It took time for me to learn that what God deems as good gifts are entirely different than what we perceive with our human understanding.

The good gift is actually the best gift God can give us—the fullness of His presence through the indwelling Holy Spirit promised by Him when we place our faith in Jesus Christ.

As our heavenly Father, God will pour out His blessings in so many unique, personal, and practical ways, but none compares to the presence of His Holy Spirit dwelling in our hearts and minds. I uncovered that truth as I leaned more into God during that time I was hurting the most. His goodness came as I developed a deep abiding relationship with Him. He held me up. Covered me with His love. Reminded me of my worth. Laid down His life for me. And cared for me as my heavenly Father.

Those years of separation from my dad actually became the time when God accomplished the most beautiful and sanctifying work on my heart and soul, as I depended on Him more than ever before. When God promises good gifts, He means it, my friend. Will you believe this truth, even if you're in a place in which it doesn't feel true?

READ

Luke 11:1-13

RESPOND

God, I believe that if I, a sinful person, can desire to give good gifts to my children (by birth, adoption, or spiritual adoption), how much more You will give the Holy Spirit when I ask it of You. Forgive me for the times I doubt Your love for me. Forgive me when I demand gifts that won't last until eternity. Help me to see You as the good Father You are as I treasure the gift of the Holy Spirit living within me. In Jesus' name, amen.

REFLECT

What does it look like to see God as your heavenly Father who is about the business of giving you the one gift you need most of all—the presence of the Holy Spirit dwelling in your soul?

29

All In

You must love the Lord your God with all your heart, all your soul, all your mind, and all your strength.

MARK 12:30

What do you think it means to love the Lord your God with all your heart, soul, mind, and strength? Yes, *all*!

While I had heard the expression "all in" tossed around in conversation, I didn't realize what it meant until I played my first card game with poker chips. With each hand, we had to decide if we were going to toss in a few chips, fold, or play "all in." In one of those strategic moves, I realized that this "all in" concept was something God was calling me to personally...not in a card game but in my faith walk.

Was I willing to be in "all in" when it came to my commitment to God? I know—tough question! What about you? Are you willing to yield to Him every part of your life, or do you feel you have to hold a bit back for yourself? What would it feel like to give Him your whole heart? Are there untouchable portions? Would you be willing to give God every inch of space in your mind, or do you categorize certain areas "nonspiritual"?

To give God everything changes everything.

Choosing to be "all in" is a risk of vulnerability before God. It's a complete surrender of our own wants, desires, and dreams. And it requires total transparency before God as we admit our inabilities, imperfections, and weaknesses. But when Jesus commands us to love God with all our heart, soul, mind, and strength, it's not just because He thinks His Father is entitled to our complete devotion; it's because He knows it's good for us too.

READ

Mark 12:28-34

RESPOND

God, I will strive to love You with all my heart, soul, mind, and strength. God, I want to be "all in" for You. Forgive me for withholding a portion of myself from You. Please give me the courage to step out in faith and surrender all to Your purposes and kingdom work. In Jesus' name, amen.

REFLECT

How is God prompting you to be "all in" for Him?

Head on over to http://www.unblindedfaith.com/find/ for free access to "Find Your Why," a great tool to help you embrace the way God made you and the purposes He has for your life.

30

This Power

When Simon saw that the Spirit was given when the apostles laid their hands on people, he offered them money to buy this power. "Let me have this power, too," he exclaimed, "so that when I lay my hands on people, they will receive the Holy Spirit!"

ACTS 8:18-19

Do you find yourself wanting what others have, especially when it comes to the way God has gifted them? Are you tempted to be a little bit manipulative or barter with God to get what you want or think you deserve?

It seems that was Simon's problem. He saw a good thing and wanted it for himself. Can we fault him for being amazed by the miracles Philip performed and in awe of the working of the Holy Spirit manifested in the works of the apostles? Haven't we coveted a particular gifting or opportunity that God ordained in someone else's life? Don't we want God's power to be at work in us? Are we hoping money, talent, and carefully crafted words will get us the results we desire? But the real question is do we want the gift more than the Giver?

What a slippery slope we can easily fall onto when we try to buy what God intended as a gift.

Simon was doing all the right things—confessing his faith in Jesus and getting baptized—but his heart was out of whack. Could the same be said for us? Are we tempted to covet power (or anything for that matter) that was never meant for us? What transpires when we allow those feelings of jealously to manifest and grow, pushing us forward and driving us into sin? Yes, it is a vicious cycle, but there is a way out. As Philip said to Simon, we must repent of our wickedness and pray to the Lord, so that He may forgive our evil thoughts before they turn into regrettable actions (Acts 8:22).

READ

Acts 8:18-25

RESPOND

God, I yield to Your power to manifest in me as I resist bitter jealousy and being held captive by sin. Please root out every bit of jealousy in me. Help me own it and practice gratitude instead. Lord, I want Your power to be at work in me, according to Your will and purposes for Your glory alone. In Jesus' name, amen.

REFLECT

In what ways are you falling into the trap of jealousy and stumbling into sin?

31

Owning Up

If we go around bragging, "We have no sin," then we are fooling ourselves and are strangers to the truth. But if we own up to our sins, God shows that He is faithful and just by forgiving us of our sins and purifying us from the pollution of all the bad things we have done.

1 JOHN 1:8-9 THE VOICE

Are you the type of person who is keenly aware of your own sin? Or are you that person sitting in the pew, listening to the pastor preaching, while elbowing the one sitting next to you? Well, the apostle John levels the playing field, saying we're fooling ourselves if we think we are without sin.

The problem is that all sin is not equally apparent. As we say in our family, "Some of our sin precedes us, like an approaching thunderstorm, and some follows quietly behind, like a shadow in the setting sun." In other words, some sin is quite obvious, like anger, while other sin is more easily disguised, like jealousy. Regardless of how we sin, it's all hard to own up to. We just don't want to admit that we did something wrong.

Without confession, sin becomes the stronghold that insidiously infects every area of our lives.

A white lie is simply the first in a litany of deception leading to the destruction of a relationship. The temptation to let your eyes wander online quickly becomes an addiction to pornography. A longing for that $50 pair of discounted jeans snowballs into overspending and using savings behind your spouse's back.

Dealing with the external manifestation of sin—the behavior—doesn't change the internal thought life in which sin takes on a mind of its own. The only way to tackle sin is to claim it for what it is—disobedience against God—and confess to God, in order to experience the freedom Christ offers through His forgiveness. Only in Christ will we get to live as forgiven sinners saved by grace.

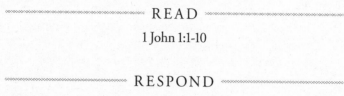

READ

1 John 1:1-10

RESPOND

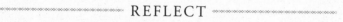

God, I choose to own up to my sin, so I can experience Your faithfulness and forgiveness purifying me from all the things I have done wrong and against Your Word. Thank You for being faithful to forgive my sin. Thank You for making a way for me to break free from my bad behavior. Clean out the pollution in my heart and make me pure in You. In Jesus' name, amen.

REFLECT

What behavior, habit, or mind-set have you made excuses for instead of owning as sin? What will it take for you to confess it before God and fully repent so that you can be free of that pollution?

32

Brand-New

Anyone who belongs to Christ has become a new person. The old life is gone; a newl ife has begun!

2 CORINTHIANS 5:17

Have you embraced the promise that when you belong to Christ, you truly have become a new person? Have you given Him your old life and embraced the new one He offers you? Or are you busy trying to clean up your life on your own, making it good enough for Him to actually do something with?

Stephen and I were barely married a year when we passed by a set of Adirondack chairs on the side of the road. He quickly pulled over and popped open our hatchback before I could object. I was mortified to pick up someone's roadside trash...until we got home.

When Stephen pulled those chairs out of the car, I could tell they were the real deal—quality-made wooden chairs that simply needed a sanding job and fresh coat of paint. That was the first castoff that made its way into our home. Over the last twenty years, we've claimed plenty of other people's trash as our treasures. With each piece of rescued décor, I'm reminded that God is about the business of redeeming our lives for His purposes. Even if someone else might consider us worthless. Even if we feel like nothing but a throwaway. God is our great Rescuer.

God takes us in any state and
re-creates our lives with glorious purpose.

He doesn't just give us a sand job and a fresh coat of paint—God literally makes us brand-new. The word *new* in this verse comes from the Greek word *kainos*, which means "recently made, fresh, recent, unworn, of a new kind, unprecedented."[3] We might feel as if He's trying to work with the old version of ourselves, but really, through our faith in Christ, it's as if He starts from scratch. Can you even get your mind around that? Imagine what would happen if we lived like the new creations He made us to be.

READ

2 Corinthians 5:11-21

RESPOND

God, I believe that since I belong to Christ, I am a new person, the old is gone and the new life has begun. It's a miracle I can't even comprehend. Increase my faith to understand Your power at work in my life. Show me how to live as that new creation for Your glory. In Jesus' name, amen.

REFLECT

Are you living like a new creation in Christ, or uselessly hanging on to the old creation you once were?

33

Love Summed Up

The commandments say, "You must not commit adultery. You must not murder. You must not steal. You must not covet." These—and other such commandments—are summed up in this one commandment: "Love your neighbor as yourself."

ROMANS 13:9

Have you ever considered how plain the commandments of God really are? And yet we struggle to heed them! I wonder, what would happen if instead of focusing on what not to do, we focused on what to do? Isn't that exactly the point Paul is making to the Romans in this verse?

But what does it actually mean to love your neighbor as yourself? First Corinthians 13 describes love as patient and kind, not jealous, boastful, proud, or rude, and not selfish, irritable, or bent on holding a grudge. So while we might not love perfectly, we can strive to control the attitude of our hearts and willingness to love in action according to these instructions, right?

But see, this command in Romans includes two very important words at the end of the sentence: "as yourself." What does it look like to apply "as yourself" action steps toward our neighbors in a way that demonstrates God's love? Should we be preparing meals for our neighbors? Hosting gatherings to build relationships? Making our homes places to open the Word together? Seeking out opportunities to serve so our neighbors might be able to rest, physically and spiritually?

Loving our neighbors as ourselves requires a kind of love in action that goes beyond the heart and moves right into our hands and feet, homes and workplaces, every single day.

In this mission to love others as we love ourselves, the real secret is in simply following Christ's example as He laid down His own life for us. Isn't that the greatest act of selfless love we've ever seen?

READ

Romans 13:8-14

RESPOND

God, I will strive to love my neighbor as myself, so I may fulfill Your commandments. Thank You for modeling what love is in the way You sacrificed Your Son on my behalf. Thank You, Jesus, for laying down Your life for me. God, please move me toward sacrificial love for my neighbors. In Jesus' name, amen.

REFLECT

How do you feel God is calling you to love your neighbor as yourself?

34

Even If

Even if that person wrongs you seven times a day and each time turns again and asks forgiveness, you must forgive.

LUKE 17:4

How do you feel about the command to forgive the person who has wronged you again and again? What if the tables are turned, and you're the one who needs to be forgiven?

Unforgiveness is like a cancer on a mission to destroy our lives.

Choosing to not forgive simply keeps the pain alive, as we remain in a place of vulnerability, replaying scenes and recounting hurts again and again. I know this victim mentality well, as I lived it for all too long. When my dad and I were not on speaking terms, I carried in my heart tremendous hurt and anger, not only because of that one horrific falling out but for a lifetime of offenses.

Instead of forgiving seventy times seven, I held on to the pain seventy times seven. Until that one day when God got ahold of my heart. He gently but boldly asked me to lay at His feet my wounds and yield to Him the outcome. He wasn't asking me to forget, but to trust Him to be fair and merciful. Even if He wasn't going to restore my relationship with my dad. Even if His justice may not feel sufficient from my perspective. Even if I would never hear "I'm sorry" from the lips of my father. I submitted, not with a wholehearted *yes* but with an *okay*.

Choosing to forgive is really an act of obedience toward God that benefits us most of all, because He takes the burden from us and gives us our life back.

As I heeded God's Word to forgive my dad, He lifted the weight of sadness from my soul. He gave me new hope and even a heart of compassion for my dad, as I daily chose to forgive him. And in the process, God enabled me to live again without the tormenting anger, shame, and feeling of rejection. I got to the place of praying for God to bless my father, even if I never saw him again, and that was when I realized I was experiencing the freedom of total forgiveness. Should we be surprised that was the day before my father reached out to me and asked for my forgiveness? Four years of silence was finally broken—not when he said, "I'm sorry. I was wrong. Will you forgive me?" but when I was able to say to him, "Yes, Dad, I forgave you long ago."

READ

Luke 17:1-10

RESPOND.

God, I will obey Your instructions to forgive those who have hurt me again and again. God, please help me forgive easily, while also trusting You as my protector. Thank You for this urging to forgive those I've been wounded by so I can heal and move forward. In Jesus' name, amen.

REFLECT

What does it look like for you to embrace the practice of forgiveness for every offense, past and present?

35

Sinner Saved

We are made right with God by placing our faith in Jesus Christ. And this is true for everyone who believes, no matter who we are. For everyone has sinned; we all fall short of God's glorious standard.

ROMANS 3:22-23

How do you think you're made right with God? What about the people you're in relationship with? And how about those folks who seem to be "good people" but end up in the middle of trouble, and those who are "bad people" but get away with everything?

Personally, I'd be thrilled if we could make the whole matter of sin simply go away. Maybe that's why I'm a fan of Hallmark movies, where I can predict the outcome and trust that the good guys will win and the bad guys will get what they have coming. But real life is more like *Persons of Interest,* a TV series that suits my husband's preference. Each episode is supposedly about rescuing innocent people from harm, but it's not quite clear who is really innocent. Even the main characters, sent out on a rescue mission, often find themselves needing to be rescued. I suppose we might be able to find out who is good and who is bad on a TV show, but we'll never figure it out in real life. That's because there is no such thing as a "good person" or "bad person," since all have sinned and fallen short of the glory of God. Yes, *all.*

Sin is woven deep into our stories, but
God's grace unravels its grip.

We have a choice of whether we'll give in to the flesh or walk in the Spirit. Or put another way—we can make a good choice or a bad choice. So although we're sinners, we don't have to keep on sinning, because we are saved by grace when we put our faith in Jesus Christ.

That's our public declaration, making us officially neither good nor bad, but rather rescued and redeemed.

READ

Romans 3:21-31

RESPOND

God, I believe my salvation comes by faith in Your Son, Jesus, and I agree that I am indeed a sinner. Thank You, God, for forgiving me of my sin and extending me Your grace and mercy. Let it not be in vain! May I live in such a way that I run from sin and live in Your grace as rescued and redeemed. In Jesus' name, amen.

REFLECT

Will you accept your true identity as a sinner saved by grace, or will you continue to live as a sinner on the run?

36

Pour Out Your Heart

O my people, trust in him at all times. Pour out your heart to him, for God is our refuge.

PSALM 62:8

What does it look like for you to trust in God at all times? Not just the times you're out of options, but all times? What about running to God with your heart, especially when you are seeking refuge, instead of turning to everyone and everything else for comfort?

My parents always told me to stop wearing my heart on my sleeve, and well, there was wisdom in that instruction. I would bare my soul to a stranger, if it meant a deep heart connection. Can you relate? Or do you prefer a buttoned-up approach? I ask only because I think how we feel about what we share with others may also reflect how honest we get with God. Think about it for a moment: Would you say your closest friends and family members are on a need-to-know basis, and basically, no one needs to know? Is that also what your relationship with God looks like? Or are you comfortable pouring out your heart to Him?

Some of us will always wear our hearts on our sleeves and others will prefer to keep them tucked nicely inside the chest cavity, as God so perfectly designed. But regardless of our willingness or hesitancy to share with a friend or stranger, we always ought to give full access to our Creator and Maker.

God is the One who most perfectly guards our hearts as He provides safe refuge for our souls.

For those of us who desire to be heard, He's the safest One to hear our words. For those of us who don't have much to say, the same is true. He is always our refuge and the One we can pour out our hearts to without fear or regret.

READ

Psalm 62:1-12

RESPOND

God, I will pour out my trust in You at all times, because You are my place of refuge. Forgive me when I place my trust elsewhere. Give me the courage and conviction to turn to You first and be honest about everything. Enable me to trust You more and more, knowing You'll always be my refuge. In Jesus' name, amen.

REFLECT

How do you feel about pouring out your heart to God and trusting Him with your deepest needs?

37

Generous Grace

He gives grace generously. As the Scriptures say,
"God opposes the proud but gives grace to the humble."

JAMES 4:6

Why do we complicate what God expects of us? Is it because we're looking at Him through the wrong set of lenses? Are we trying to meet a standard that's been placed upon us by others rather than submitting to the one God has given us?

Some might say that God's expectations are too high. That resisting the devil and the desires of our flesh is more than we should have to endure (James 4:7). That doing the right thing isn't necessarily relevant these days. But does God ask us to do what is beyond our ability?

Is it really that hard to be humble before Him and receive His generous grace? What is keeping us from washing our hands of sin, purifying our hearts, and being loyal to God alone (James 4:8)? In our flesh, we will fail to do what God asks of us, but He's not required us to operate in our flesh.

> Through Jesus Christ, we receive the power and presence of the Holy Spirit, who is always at work in us, guiding us in what is good, right, and pure.

But will we agree with His truth and humbly heed His call so we may experience His grace in full?

READ

James 4:1-10

RESPOND

God, I believe You give grace generously, because the Scriptures say You oppose the proud but give grace to the humble. Thank You for Your generous grace. Thank You for enabling me to fulfill Your commands by heeding the work of the Holy Spirit. May I long for Your ways more than mine. In Jesus' name, amen.

REFLECT

In what ways is God calling you to embrace His generous grace and walk humbly in His ways?

38

Gathering Together

Let us not neglect our meeting together, as some people do, but encourage one another, especially now that the day of his return is drawing near.

HEBREWS 10:25

Are you tempted to forsake gathering together with other Christians? Maybe skip church? Or avoid a small group or Bible study commitment?

Even as an extrovert, there are times I want to withdraw from community life. It's not that being with people taps me out, but rather that doing life together can sometimes be so messy, making me want to run for the hills. Can you relate? But that desire to run doesn't mean we should give in to it.

We often need to dive into community knowing that God is about the business of accomplishing His work even in the midst of our mess. I learned that lesson on a Sunday when I was tempted to skip church after a week of travel but remembered I promised to bring a side dish to small group meeting after service. Without a valid out, I kicked it into high gear and we barely made it to church on time. I sat through the sermon arguing with God about the value of showing up, since my heart wasn't in it, but got no answer at all...until the end of our small group time. The topic from the sermon combined with the video we watched in our group spurred on an authentic time of sharing. One couple finally let their pain come to the surface and boldly asked for support. We gathered around them and prayed for God's healing and leading. The relief on their faces proved to me that encouragement is something that can only happen when we show up.

Simply by gathering together,
we become an encouragement to each other.

Should we be surprised that such a little act of obedience could reap such a blessing?

READ

Hebrews 10:19-39

RESPOND

God, I will not neglect meeting together with my brothers and sisters in Christ, so I may be an encourager and receive encouragement. Please forgive me for my stubbornness and the times I run from what You say is best. Give me the conviction and courage to heed Your Word, especially when it comes to gathering together with my brothers and sisters in Christ. In Jesus' name, amen.

REFLECT

What does it look like for you to not forsake gathering together with believers, even if being fully present is simply an act of obedience to God?

39

Wait Patiently

Wait patiently for the Lord*. Be brave and courageous. Yes, wait patiently for the* Lord*.*

PSALM 27:14

How do you handle waiting on God? Do you feel brave and courageous, or timid and afraid? I confess that I'm a hot mess when it comes to waiting on anyone or anything, even if it is God Himself. *Impatient* ought to be my middle name, because I want to hurry up every process and find a solution. Sound familiar?

In one season of waiting, I felt the Lord ask me to lay down my ministry completely. Was I crushed and confused? Absolutely!

While a season of waiting may feel purposeless, it's likely that God is using it to prepare us for what is yet to come.

From this vantage point years later, I can see how God orchestrated the details so I could savor the year of homeschooling my daughter and experience deep Scripture study with a friend.

God invites us to do so much while we wait on Him, which David illustrates so clearly in this particular psalm. While he was waiting on God, his heart was actually moved to prayer and connecting with Him on a deeper level (Psalm 27:7-8). Think about the last time you waited on the Lord. Did you find yourself drawing toward Him, even if you were pleading your case again and again?

Like David, we may find that times of waiting on God provides a space for Him to accomplish a great work in our lives.

READ

Psalm 27:1-14

RESPOND

God, I will wait patiently for You, while growing braver and more courageous, as I watch for Your purposes to prevail. I confess it is so hard to wait, and especially to wait patiently. Lord, change my perspective on waiting, so I may look for Your work instead of fretting over the outcome. Build my trust muscle, Lord. In Jesus' name, amen.

REFLECT

How can you embrace the process of waiting on God patiently with brave and courageous faith?

Head on over to http://www.unblindedfaith.com/inspired/ to download a set of Scripture cards to use as you wait on the Lord and practice pouring out your heart to Him.

40

Preparing to Endure

Prepare your minds for action and exercise self-control. Put all your hope in the gracious salvation that will come to you when Jesus Christ is revealed to the world.

1 PETER 1:13

What does it look like for you to prepare your mind for action and embrace the practice of exercising self-control? If this is something you choose to be intentional about in the little things, could it also be a way to prepare for the more challenging times when you face temptations and trials (1 Peter 1:7)?

While I've been through my fair share of trials, I really didn't think about the benefit of striving to prepare in advance for them through readying my mind for action and practicing self-control. It sort of always felt like, "Well, we'll just deal when the drama hits again." But then I became a bystander to my daughters' self-imposed sugar fast. Their goal was to abstain from sugar for one week for the sake of breaking their self-confessed addiction. My middle daughter does not like feeling controlled by anyone or anything, which makes being her mama quite the challenge, but it's a pretty awesome trait when it comes to exercising self-control.

While their attempt to avoid all things that contained sugar made fixing even breakfast stressful, and quite frankly, it annoyed me, I did come to see the benefit to their spiritual development. They had to engage their minds to assess truth from fiction as they strived to stick with their plan. Isn't that what we need to do in a trial?

In our world of instant gratification, exercising self-control is a necessity for building spiritual endurance.

When we put our self-control muscles to work in everyday ordinary tasks, we're prepping our minds to work hard, long, fast, and furiously against the temptations that will come our way. So maybe we ought to ask God to show us what simple, insignificant thing He might want us to fast from in order to exercise our self-control muscle as a way of disciplining our minds and hearts for the spiritual race ahead.

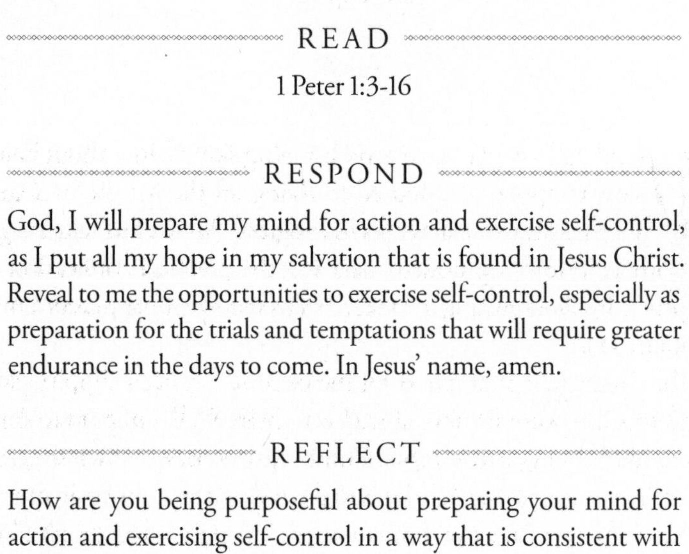

READ

1 Peter 1:3-16

RESPOND

God, I will prepare my mind for action and exercise self-control, as I put all my hope in my salvation that is found in Jesus Christ. Reveal to me the opportunities to exercise self-control, especially as preparation for the trials and temptations that will require greater endurance in the days to come. In Jesus' name, amen.

REFLECT

How are you being purposeful about preparing your mind for action and exercising self-control in a way that is consistent with God's Word?

41

Quick. Slow. Slow.

Understand this, my dear brothers and sisters: You must all be quick to listen, slow to speak, and slow to get angry.

JAMES 1:19

Would you say you have good listening skills? How about being slow to speak, as opposed to flying off the handle in anger? Take heart; we're all works in progress. Some of us take longer than others in learning how to walk out the practical application of Scripture. It's like learning a dance...steps require more practice over the long haul.

The dance metaphor works for me because I've been clippity-clopping across the wooden floor since I was three. Well, I'm not tap dancing anymore, but I do love a good Zumba fitness class—which is a great way to be reminded how hard it is to learn even the most basic move.

Much to my dismay, and my mother's, my poor knees didn't allow my Rockette dream to ever become a reality. My mom hoped I'd at least marry a man who liked to dance; that didn't pan out either, although she tried. Right after we got engaged, she gave us a gift certificate for ballroom dance lessons just so Stephen could spin me around the floor at our wedding. Poor guy! He begrudgingly worked his way through those lessons, while I dreamed of a life in which he'd twirl me around the kitchen after dinner...quick...slow...slow...dip. *Ahem.* Not so much. The man has danced with me all of four times since our wedding, but who's counting? I'd rather have a husband living out the quick, slow, slow of Scripture over moves on a dance floor any day.

Have you ever considered the steps the God of the Universe choreographed for us to make our relationships thrive?

Quick to listen. Is there anything more valuable to intimacy in a relationship than the feeling of being heard?

Slow to speak. As my father would say, "loose lips sink ships." Yes, not everything we think must come out of our mouths. How wise it is to slow down our words to spare unnecessary hurt!

Slow to get angry. Count to three. Take a deep breath. Open up your palms and let go of that anger. Whatever it takes, friend, wouldn't you agree that taking our temper down a notch or two is good for everyone involved?

Imagine if you let God take the lead and set the rhythms of your relationship style motion—quick...slow...slow, and maybe a dip into pure joy.

READ

James 1:19-27

RESPOND

God, I will be quick to listen, slow to speak, and slow to get angry. Thank You for Your instructions, Lord, designed to preserve the relationships You've called me to be in. Forgive me when I refuse to do what You've clearly shown is best. Give me humility to walk in step with Your leading. In Jesus' name, amen.

REFLECT

In what ways do you need to work on being quick to listen, slow to speak, and slow to get angry?

42

Awesome and Impartial

For the Lord your God is God of gods and Lord of lords, the great, the mighty, and the awesome God, who is not partial and takes no bribe.

DEUTERONOMY 10:17 ESV

Do you believe that God is great and mighty, awesome and impartial? Or do you think He is biased and unjust, willing to take bribes?

Before I began reading Scripture for myself, I imagined God as a cosmic genie or Santa Claus, prepared to dole out spells and gifts according to behavior. In my mind, He was a giver and a taker, and it was all based on performance. I was looking at God through the lens of what I experienced in my earthly relationships rather than the truth of Scripture. I believed if I could be good enough, God would love me *just* enough. Have you fallen into this belief pattern too?

God can't love you or me any more or less than He already does today (Psalm 89:33).

He doesn't love someone else any more or any less than He loves you. He doesn't love you any less just because you've messed up. He doesn't love you more because you rocked the world today.

Although we're guilty of trying, we cannot bribe God under any circumstance. The heavens, the earth, and everything in between belongs to God (Deuteronomy 10:14). What could we give Him that He doesn't already own?

READ

Deuteronomy 10:12-22

RESPOND

God, I believe You are great and mighty, awesome and impartial. I also believe that You do not take bribes. Forgive me when I try to earn Your love. Forgive me when I doubt Your love. Help me walk in faith, trusting in who You say You are. In Jesus' name, amen.

REFLECT

What does it look like to live according to the truth of who God says He is and not according to your misconceptions and misunderstandings?

43

The Potter's Hands

What sorrow awaits those who argue with their Creator. Does a clay pot argue with its maker? Does the clay dispute with the one who shapes it, saying, "Stop, you're doing it wrong!" Does the pot exclaim, "How clumsy can you be?"

ISAIAH 45:9

Do you ever wonder about what God was up to when He was busy creating you? Do you find yourself questioning whether He messed up?

In my early twenties, I had the opportunity to take a pottery class with my friend at the local university. After a semester of practice, we thought we knew enough to set out on our own and worked out a deal to use the studio on campus to perfect our craft in exchange for supervising student use of the space. For weeks upon weeks, we showed up, determined to become accomplished potters. Alas, the progression never came.

To create a beautiful clay vessel, you have to start with the right kind of clay. *Kind of like how we are all different within the body of Christ and not meant for the same purpose.* Next, you get rid of all the air bubbles in the clay by repeatedly throwing it down on a solid surface before slamming it onto the wheel, making sure you get good suction. *A bit like the sanctification process we go through to become more like Christ.* Sitting in the proper—and most uncomfortable—leaned-over position, you bear your weight onto the clay to center it. *How often does God allow uncomfortable, stretching, pressure-filled life experiences to transform us into His perfect vessel?* Finally, you pull and push against the clay to create the shape you had in mind. *Ah, more sanctification leading to transformation.* When it's the shape you desire, you cut it from the wheel with a wire and let it dry before moving on to the next stages of carving the foot and glazing before firing in the kiln. *Sanctification continues.*

Want to know what all my efforts effort resulted in? My masterpiece—an itsy bitsy bowl fit for holding a tea light candle. It wasn't exactly what I had in mind, but how I've treasured that little vessel simply because I made it.

> Imagine how the Master Potter treasures us, His masterpieces, because He's skillfully and purposefully shaped us into His vessels.

We all look different. We all fulfill a unique need. Yet we're all made through a similar process. He knows where to push and pull on our hearts to make us into the vessels He had in mind before we took our first breath. He knows the glaze that best suits us as well as the firing temperature that won't cause us to implode in the kiln. Yes, God is the Master Potter who knows what He's doing with His clay.

READ

Isaiah 45:9-13

RESPOND

God, I choose to believe You are my Creator and knew what You were doing when You made me. Thank You for being the Master Potter who shaped me into a unique and precious vessel. Lord, forgive me for doubting Your design. Open my eyes to see the ways You're working in me to refine me and accomplish Your purpose in my life for Your glory. In Jesus' name, amen.

REFLECT

How is God leading you to embrace His work as the Master Potter, who carefully formed you and shaped your life?

44

Truth in Love

We will speak the truth in love, growing in every way more and more like Christ, who is the head of his body, the church.

EPHESIANS 4:15

What do you think it means to speak the truth in love? How can doing so be part of the growth process in becoming more like Christ?

A counselor once said to me that we're only as healthy as the secrets we keep. Her words struck me to the core as I realized the damage to my soul over the secrets I was forced to keep as a child. Those secrets are probably why I'm so passionate about authenticity in all my relationships. I'm the type of gal who will put it on the table for the sake of living in the truth instead of lies. But I've also had to learn that speaking the truth in love doesn't mean expressing every single opinion and sharing every gory detail.

When the grace of God works its way through our hearts first, His unchanging truth can be fully delivered with love.

Only then can we reach toward that brother or sister in Christ with a heart tender to the Lord's leading, to serve as His hands and feet. The goal isn't to make much or little of sin, but rather to make a safe place for conviction to set in so that the Holy Spirit can do the Lord's work.

Speaking the truth in love requires approaching a particularly challenging conversation with the delicate balance of humility and integrity. It also requires paying attention to the timing of what we say for the sake of the recipient's ability to process and receive the truth, along with considering nearby listeners.

When we seek to give God the space to accomplish His purposes through using us to speak the truth, He'll be the one to move in us with His grace and by the power of His love.

READ

Ephesians 4:1-16

RESPOND

God, I will speak the truth in love, so I may grow in every way more like Christ. Jesus, thank You for being our example for speaking the truth in love. Lord, please give me courage and sensitivity to follow Your example. May my passion for truth not outweigh Your measure of grace fueled entirely by Your love. In Jesus' name, amen.

REFLECT

As you seek to speak the truth, would you also be willing to ask God to fill your heart with His love so you communicate with discernment, wisdom, and grace to the hearer?

45

Holy Purpose

It will be your mission to open their eyes so that they may turn from darkness to light and from the kingdom of Satan to the kingdom of God. This is so that they may receive forgiveness of all their sins and have a place among those who are set apart for a holy purpose through having faith in Me.

ACTS 26:18 THE VOICE

Have you ever considered how the kingdom of God is represented by light while the kingdom of Satan is defined by darkness? Light and darkness cannot exist together, because the light always chases out the darkness. Imagine going into a pitch-black room and turning on a flashlight—that light now eradicates the darkness effortlessly. But go into a brightly lit room and try to make it dark; it's practically impossible without shutting down every source of light. Isn't this the reality of our faith? We get to choose if we want to live in the light or in the darkness.

The Light is for us, because Christ is for life.

Christ is the light of the world. He shines into the darkness and shows us our deeds for what they are—God's greatest heartbreak (John 8:12). He reveals our sin-stained hands even if we're still denying that we've turned our backs on God, shut down His call, and resisted His leading. His light breaks through the darkness where we hide our sin and shame and our addictions become our strongholds. In the darkness we deceive ourselves into believing that our conduct is unseen and our actions don't have consequences because we're better than so-and-so. Because we don't struggle with *this* and *that*.

We don't end up in the darkness accidentally. We choose to go there purposefully, but Jesus graciously, kindly, and boldly offers a way out. We have the choice to step into the light, where the kingdom of God exists. Where forgiveness abounds. Where holy purpose grows for kingdom glory.

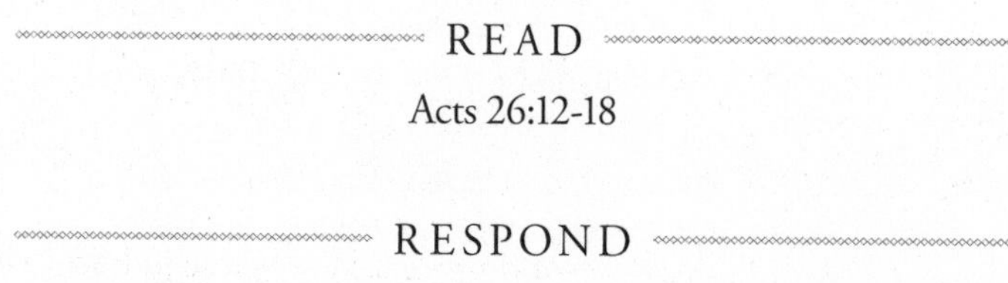

READ

Acts 26:12-18

RESPOND

God, I believe You can open my eyes and turn me from darkness to light, from the kingdom of Satan to Your kingdom, through receiving Your forgiveness and accepting the places set apart for me with holy purpose found in Jesus Christ. Forgive me for staying in the dark for too long and for returning to its shelter when I ought to have run to the light. God, please give me the courage to confess my sin to You and to turn in repentance, running steadfastly into the light. In Jesus' name, amen.

REFLECT

Is it time to ask God to set afresh in you a holy purpose in Jesus Christ, leading you away from the darkness and giving you the grace and courage to live in the light?

46

The Thief Is Real

The thief comes only to steal and kill and destroy.

JOHN 10:10 NIV

Have you experienced the workings of a thief? Do you know what it is like to be stolen from? To have your life turned upside down with the intent of destruction? I hope your answer is no. Unfortunately, my answer is yes.

I was sitting across from my friend, engrossed in conversation, when I felt my phone vibrate. My husband wanted to know why I'd just charged $800, as he received a notification by text from the credit card company. I reach down into my purse to grab my wallet, only to discover that it was missing. Stolen by a thief who was prowling around waiting for a naïve woman to forget about her purse at the foot of her chair (tucked under her coat), so she (caught on camera but escaped arrest) could charge nearly $5,000 in less than 30 minutes by buying gift cards at area super stores!

The next few hours were total chaos, as I called the police, the bank, and the credit card companies, and tried to recall every item in my wallet. What a hassle! But more than the inconvenience was the sense of violation I felt, along with an overwhelming sense of fear. I lost more than my wallet from the Thief, who was not a "she" but rather the Enemy of God who masquerades, deceives, and is so cunning we often don't see his work (2 Corinthians 11:14).

Make no mistake, Satan is always busy at work.

He is messing with you, prowling around like a roaring lion seeking to destroy, but he doesn't get the last say (1 Peter 5:8). We get to decide how we'll respond to his attacks. I could have easily grown bitter and paralyzed in fear. But instead, God moved me to forgive Satan's minion and refuse to quake in my boots any longer, remembering that my security, identity, and peace is found in Christ alone.

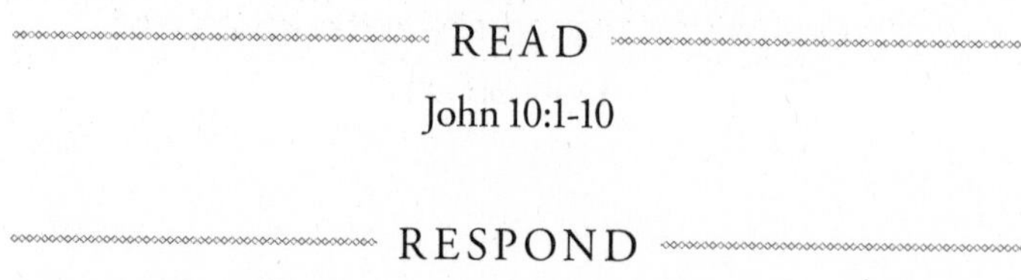

READ

John 10:1-10

RESPOND

God, I believe the Thief comes to steal, kill, and destroy. Make me more aware of how real the battle is in the spiritual realm. God, help me fight against the Enemy's attacks and not give in to them. Let me not partner with the works of the Enemy in any way but be fully committed to walking in obedience according to Your Word. In Jesus' name, amen.

REFLECT

What if your feet hit the floor each day with such faith and focus on the Lord that the Enemy said, "Oh, no, she's awake and ready for battle!" and chose to leave you alone?

47

Better Quantity and Quality

I have come that they may life, and have it to the full.

JOHN 10:10 NIV

How often do we quote only half a verse—you know, the half that feels good? Isn't that what we do with this half of John 10:10? We go around declaring that God promises us a full, abundant life, as though He's ready to drop an overstuffed sack full of gifts at our fireplace. Oh, yes, our God is a good Father who gives good gifts to His children (James 1:17). For that we can be so very grateful. But the full life God promises us is not material prosperity, even though He is the One who distributes such blessings. The fullness of life that we truly crave is the fullness that comes through Jesus Christ Himself!

That word, *full*, in Greek is *perissos*, which means, "in the sense of beyond; superabundantly (in quantity) or superior (in quality)."[4] Take that in for a minute.

The life Jesus offers us is of better quantity and quality than we'll find in anyone or anything else.

Yes, friends, there is a Thief. He is after us. But there is a God who is for us. And He wins every time. I can attest to that. I lived the first half of my life without Jesus, and I promise you, life with Him as my Lord is so much better—not because I have more success or financial security, better health or overall strength. On the contrary! Choosing to believe in Jesus as my Savior has required sacrificing the things I once held so dear—a big career, an expensive lifestyle, fancy titles, exotic vacations. I'm not saying the fullness of Christ is a matter of the haves and have-nots, but rather that our definition of success doesn't always line up to God's. The fullness Christ offers isn't about our "stuff" nor our experiences—it's about what we find as we uncover a kind of unshakable purpose and peace, hope and joy, through His overflowing love and grace poured out on our life.

READ

John 1:10-21

RESPOND

God, I believe Jesus has come so I may have life to the full. Please redefine for me what that fullness looks like as I grow wiser against the Enemy's attacks. Show me how to embrace the fullness You provide and live for Your glory. In Jesus' name, amen.

REFLECT

How have you experienced the fullness of God in your life, in spite of the Enemy's efforts?

48

The Distress Cry

In my distress I cried out to the Lord; yes, I cried to my God for help. He heard me from his sanctuary; my cry reached his ears.

2 SAMUEL 22:7

Have you ever been in a distressing situation where you felt there was no way out? Where the pain was paralyzing and the burden was too heavy to carry? Well, it may be interesting to you that in this particular verse, the word *distress* in Greek actually means "tight place."[5] The first thing that comes to my mind is the trash compactor scene in *Star Wars IV*. Was that scene as traumatic for you as it was for me? I often refer to it when I feel trapped, or in a tight place, anxious that there's no way out. Can you relate?

When I feel overwhelmed and distressed, I usually waffle back and forth between trying to control the situation and bartering with God to find a way out. That's why I find it so remarkable that this particular verse describes how David had the courage to turn to God, even though his distress was a result of his blatant sin of adultery (read 2 Samuel 11). Maybe he was so desperate for God's intervention because he epically failed when he took matters into his own hands—*ahem*, chose to murder his adulteress's husband (2 Samuel 11:15).

How often we run from God when the very thing we ought to do is cry out to Him in our distress, even if we made the mess.

Oh, yes, David made a mess, but even so he turned to the One in whom he had full confidence—the Lord as his Rock, Fortress, Savior, Protector, Shield, and Refuge (2 Samuel 22:1-3). Maybe we'd be quicker to run to God in our distress, rather than taking matters into our own hands, if we really knew the fullness of His character and the wholeness of His promises.

READ

2 Samuel 22:1-7

RESPOND

God, when I find myself in distress, I will cry out to You for help, because You will hear me. Thank You for being a God who is faithful and trustworthy. Thank You that Your Word promises Your character will never change, so I can put my trust in You. Please, Lord, cause me to cry out to You when I find myself in distress rather than taking matters into my own hands. In Jesus' name, amen.

REFLECT

What would be the benefit of crying out to God the next time you face distress, instead of taking matters into your own hands?

49

Anything and Everything

Don't worry about anything; instead, pray about everything. Tell God what you need, and thank him for all he has done. Then you will experience God's peace, which exceeds anything we can understand. His peace will guard your hearts and minds as you live in Christ Jesus.

PHILIPPIANS 4:6-7

Do you naturally take your worrisome thoughts and turn them into prayers? Do you tell God what you need and thank Him for all He has done? Because, my friend, God promises that if we talk to Him about everything, He'll give us a kind of peace that exceeds anything we can ever understand. Imagine that—a peace that guards our hearts and minds as we live in Christ Jesus.

When we give God our worry, He gives us peace in return!

In posture of surrender, choosing to trust God with His perfect plan and provisions, we receive His gift of peace. It really is freeing to trust God with it all. He gets to decide what to do with our pleas. He gets to determine which questions to answer. He gets to respond to our prayers as He goes about the business of accomplishing His purposes.

My "surrender" prayers often sound like "Heavenly Father, thank You for this day. I give it to You and ask You to order it according to Your purposes. Show me Your work that I might join You in it." I often continue with specific thanks and praises, before launching into petitions, such as "Lord, will You please show me...guide me...help me... explain to me...and do this..." I'll even ask God the tough "why" questions, because who wants to ignore the elephant in the room? Rather than squeezing around the uncomfortable unknowing, why not pursue God hard for answers?

Friend, even if it doesn't make sense in our earthly understanding, it's worth the effort to devote time to prayer. God doesn't require of us anything that isn't good for us. So His command to pray is something we should simply obey.

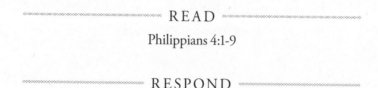

READ

Philippians 4:1-9

RESPOND

God, I will strive to not worry about anything but instead pray about everything as I tell You what I need and thank You for all You have done, so that I may experience a peace that will guard my heart and mind in Christ Jesus. Lord, thank You for giving me a way to deal with my anxiety, worry, and fear—through giving You everything that consumes my thoughts. In Jesus' name, amen.

REFLECT

How might you go about developing a consistent prayer time devoted to talking honestly with God about the things consuming your heart and mind?

Head on over to http://www.unblindedfaith.com/prayer/ to grab a free printable bookmark full of prayer prompts to place in your Bible and help you get honest with God about anything and everything.

50

Put on Your New Self

You are ready to put on your new self, modeled after the very likeness of God: truthful, righteous, and holy.

EPHESIANS 4:24 THE VOICE

Can you pinpoint how your new nature is different than your old one? What does your old self look like? Sound like? Act like? Does she come out when you're with your family of origin? Isn't it amazing how *that* fourteen-year-old, eye-rolling, insecure girl emerges out of nowhere?

Even though I was desperately trying to live as a new creation, the old me was alive and kicking for a decade after I put my faith in Jesus as Lord. No matter how much time I spent in prayer, reading Scripture, and attending Bible study, my old self—a rebellious, critical, and angry woman—continued to dominate my life. One morning when I was pleading with God to "get rid of my anger," He whispered to my heart, "It's up to you. You're wearing your anger like an old, matted fur coat. It stinks and it's heavy, yet you're too afraid to take it off, because you think it's protecting you. But it's not."

In that moment, I made a commitment to the Lord to take off that old coat—my old nature—and put on my new identity in Christ once and for all. Trust me, I felt totally naked. To take off my old familiar self meant I was completely exposed and felt utterly defenseless. But it also meant I was unhindered by the burden I had carried for too long—my past and my pain.

God will accomplish His work in us, but He requires our wholehearted cooperation and participation!

As I heeded God's urging to live as holy and righteous, wearing my new nature, I was finally able to walk forward in faith, letting go of the familiar comforts that never did protect me, and trusting God in a fresh new way to be my protector, provider, and source of peace. I make it sound like the transformation happened overnight, but in reality it was years in the making, built upon the study of Scripture, the help of counseling, and tackling my root issues buried deep in my heart. Yet it was through one powerful conversation with God that it all came together.

READ

Ephesians 4:17-31

RESPOND

God, I will put on my new self, modeled after Your very likeness. Thank You for making me into a new person through faith in Jesus Christ. Please show me where I am hanging onto the past and not trusting in Your provisions. Give me the courage to let go and lean in to the new thing You're doing in me and through me. In Jesus' name, amen.

REFLECT

What is God asking you to take off so you can put on your new identity in Christ?

51

What Time I Am Afraid

What time I am afraid, I will trust in thee.

PSALM 56:3 KJV

What do you do when you're afraid? Do you run to earthly security or choose to cling to God's promises?

The process of learning how to trust God instead of living in fear began when my oldest daughter entered kindergarten. Now don't misunderstand; I wasn't afraid of her going to school. I don't think I even cried when she got on that bus for the first time.

My fears were more about something bad happening, like an accident, illness, or unavoidable trauma. It was the kind of fear that grabbed me by the throat, causing my mind to race with irrational thoughts. While it never stopped me from living and functioning, it required a determined effort on my part to get a grip on those fears and yield them to God. So you can imagine how I had a good chuckle when Leah came home with the ABC Bible verses assignment and shared with me the one she got assigned to memorize? "W: What time I am afraid, I will trust in thee." Yep, the King James version at its finest.

To this day, if you say "afraid" in our home, there's only one go-to response: Our hands go up in the air as we shape a W with our fingers and chant the verse together. Over a decade later, the fear is not gone, but at least I know what to do with it.

Trusting in the Lord isn't about changing the outcome. It's about learning to trust God with the outcome, no matter what.

When we're afraid of that unfounded attack, we can choose to trust in the Lord. When we're afraid the commission check won't be enough, we can trust in the Lord. When we are afraid we'll make the wrong decision, we can trust in the Lord. When we're afraid of that diagnosis, we can still trust in the Lord. *What time we are afraid, we will trust thee, O Lord.*

READ

Psalm 56:1-5

RESPOND

God, when I am afraid, I will put my trust in You. Please draw me deeper into Your Word, so that I may remember Your promises when I am afraid. Help me trust You by recounting who You are and what You've already done on my behalf. In Jesus' name, amen.

REFLECT

What does it look like to put your trust in God and embrace His promises instead of living in fear?

52

A Secret Purpose

In him we were also chosen, having been predestined according to the plan of him who works out everything in conformity with the purpose of his will, in order that we, who were the first to put our hope in Christ, might be for the praise of his glory.

EPHESIANS 1:11-12 NIV

Is it hard for you to believe that you are chosen by God according to His will? Do you struggle with that promise, thinking, *Well, God may have a plan, but I don't have a clue about His purpose*?

It's so easy to feel our plans and sense of purpose should go hand in hand, but in reality, they may not even exist in the same universe. I discovered this one summer when I planned to savor every moment with my family. Before school let out, I blocked off days on the calendar for staycation togetherness. I scaled back my work to-do list. I put off some dream projects. I was certain having a plan shaped by the values God impressed upon my heart must be part of His purpose for my summer. But then nothing went according to my plan. The girls' work schedule obliterated the vacation days. I ended up consumed by my own work project, and for the bazillion hours I invested, it seemed to amount to nothing (at least from this present vantage point).

Were my plans not God's plans? Did I have a purposeless summer, since it didn't go according to plan? One might think so, right? But see, God's great purposes for my life and yours have little to do with our plans.

His purposes are about what He's working out according to His plan.

Looking back I can see how God used the "unplanned" moments

according to His kingdom purposes—like long heart-to-heart conversations with my girl as she walked through a difficult season. Hosting a Friday morning fellowship that forged deep relationships through time spent sharing and diving into Scripture. Becoming the gathering place for friends rather than jaunting around in staycation adventures.

It seems that God's purposes were people focused rather than plan honoring. But then again, isn't that in line with what God wants for us—to live as His chosen children sharing our hope in Christ and giving Him all the glory?

READ

Ephesians 1:11-23

RESPOND

God, I believe I am chosen by You, having been predestined according to Your plan that You work out in conformity with the purpose of Your will. And because I put my hope in Christ, may I bring You praise and glory. Forgive me when I neglect the simple call to proclaim Your hope. May I have my mission set on glorifying You instead of striving to find my purpose in a worldly plan. In Jesus' name, amen.

REFLECT

How is God inviting you to embrace His purposes more than pinpointing His plans, as you surrender and embrace the work He is accomplishing in you and through you for the praise of His glory?

53

Constant Conversation

Pray continually.

1 THESSALONIANS 5:17 NIV

What do you think God really means by instructing us to pray continually? Does He mean every second of every day? Are we really supposed to pray without ceasing (1 Thessalonians 5:17 KJV)?

Well, the original Greek word for *continually* is *adialeíptōs* which means, "without intermission, incessantly, without ceasing." [6] So how do we go about our days and fulfill our responsibilities but stay in constant prayer? How can we engage in conversation with others while remaining in a posture of prayer before God?

Maybe the answer is found in redefining what we think of as prayer, which translated from the Greek means to "pray to God, supplicate, worship, pray earnestly for, make a prayer." [7]

Prayer happens when we bring our needs before God and also wait to see Him provide.

Prayer happens when we lift our voices to the Lord, all by ourselves or in a gathering of brothers and sisters in Christ. Prayer is also about quieting our minds to hear His voice, listening to the Holy Spirit bring alive His Word in our hearts.

Prayer happens when we confess our sins before God and ask for His forgiveness, and also when we receive His forgiveness and live free of the guilt and shame. Prayer happens when we plead for a need on behalf of someone else, speaking words they can't even groan. Prayer happens when we continue to look for God's will to be done.

Prayer can happen anywhere and anytime. When we open up a journal and write out our thoughts along with Scripture and turn them into the cry of our hearts. When we talk to God on our walk or while driving the car. When we speak out our requests to God.

Anytime and anywhere we pause to praise God, thank God, confess our hearts to God, and wait on God, we're in the posture of prayer.

READ

1 Thessalonians 5:12-28

RESPOND

God, I will pray continually, because You tell me to do so. Please forgive me for neglecting to pray in light of all of the simple ways I can connect and communicate with You. Make me sensitive to the needs around me, so I may intercede in prayer for others. In Jesus' name, amen.

REFLECT

How can you be more intentional about praying continually, in light of all the different ways you can enter into prayer?

54

You Are More Valuable

What is the price of two sparrows—one copper coin? But not a single sparrow can fall to the ground without your Father knowing it. And the very hairs on your head are all numbered. So don't be afraid; you are more valuable to God than a whole flock of sparrows.

MATTHEW 10:29-31

How do you put a modern-day price on the value of a sparrow or a copper coin? Or could it be that Jesus was making a point about the Father's attentiveness and not the financial value of a sparrow?

I think we get tripped up over wanting to know what the sparrow is worth. But the real emphasis Jesus was making was that even if that sparrow were worth nothing, our heavenly Father takes notice. In the same regard, He considers every single hair on our heads (and even the ones that used to be there before they grayed or fell out).

Nothing God created is beyond His continual and attentive sovereign care.

God pays attention to the details, always. We don't have to be afraid of anything or anyone, because His eyes are upon us at all times, even when we stumble and fall. Even when we can't seem to catch our breath in the chaos. Even when we sit perched waiting for the next big break instead of enjoying this momentary blessing. Even when we turn our backs and run from the love the God of the universe has set aside to satisfy our souls.

Yes, God sees. He knows. He cares. Our little minds can't seem to get around the bigness of God's presence and radically love-drenched purposes. Whether it is a whole flock of sparrows or one solitary daughter of the Most High God, sitting there wondering about her purpose, God cares equally.

READ

Matthew 10:28-42

RESPOND

God, I believe You will not let a single sparrow fall to the ground without taking notice. You even know the number of all the hairs on my head. So I do not need to be afraid, because I am more valuable to You than a whole flock of sparrows. God, forgive me for forgetting to find my worth in You. Help me, God, to remember that You see me, know me, and have Your hand on my life. In Jesus' name, amen.

REFLECT

How does believing you're incredibly valued by God change the way you think of your purpose?

55

Sufficiently Full

My God will liberally supply (fill until full) your every need according to His riches in glory in Christ Jesus.

PHILIPPIANS 4:19 AMP

What do you think it means for God to fulfill your every need according to His riches in glory in Christ Jesus? Does it mean everything we see as a need, He promises to meet? Or does God's economy require us to translate our needs through His currency?

One of our weaknesses as first-world Christians is that our definition of need is so very different from how God defines it. We pray for more income, forgetting how God provided just in time for that last bill. We seek the Lord for more joy, not counting the moment of laughter we just had. We beg for a greater impact in our ministries, jobs, relationships, not recognizing the growth so far.

We want what we think we need, while neglecting to see what we already received. We lack spiritual eyesight because we've lost the art of passing down the biblical narrative from one generation to the next. Yes, we have Sunday school class, powerful sermons, and great Bible studies in which we hear stories from Scripture. But that content often settles in through the channel of head knowledge rather than filling our hearts with digestible God truths.

It's time we gather around our tables, circle up as families, and tell the next generation about what great things God has for us.

It doesn't need to be a formal undertaking, but it wouldn't hurt to take our cues from the Jewish people who are still using celebrations like the Passover meal to recount the stories of God's faithfulness. The whole meal is built around recounting Bible stories, utilizing prayers and songs as part of the narrative, with each element served on the Passover plate pointing to the truth of God's Word fulfilled by Jesus Christ. Of course, they don't know it's the Messiah who has already come! When they sing *dayenu*, a Hebrew word meaning "God will be enough. He is sufficient," they don't know His sufficiency has been delivered.[8] Imagine if we, as Christians, told the story of God's sufficiency fulfilled with the provision of Christ our Lord, not only in song and Scripture but in telling how we've seen the Godhead manifested in our very own lives. Would that change how we, and the next generation, understand God's promises?

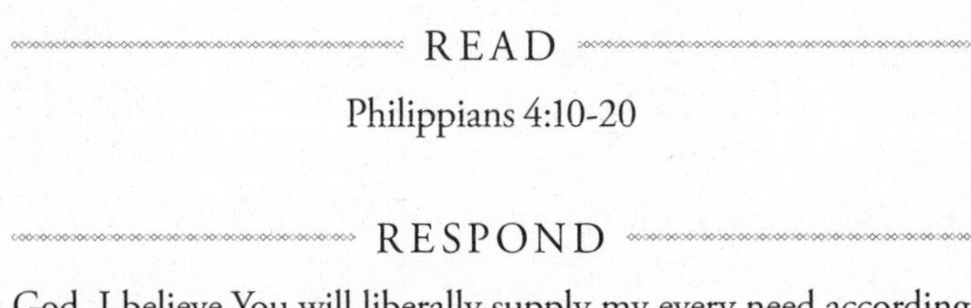

READ

Philippians 4:10-20

RESPOND

God, I believe You will liberally supply my every need according to Your riches in glory in Jesus Christ. Thank You for all Your provisions. Forgive me when I neglect to notice all the ways You've taken care of my needs. Open my eyes to see how You are already sufficient and prompt me to pass down the story of Your faithfulness to the next generation. In Jesus' name, amen.

REFLECT

How has God already supplied all your needs in Christ Jesus, even if you find yourself looking elsewhere?

56

Approved by God

We speak as messengers approved by God to be entrusted with the Good News. Our purpose is to please God, not people. He alone examines the motives of our hearts.

1 THESSALONIANS 2:4

Are there times you find yourself seeking the approval of man instead of God? Are you worried about what others might say of you? Does your fear of rejection keep you from boldly stepping out and sharing the good news?

In my family, we seem to share a common desire for the approval of others. My husband and I look back with regret, recognizing the times we avoided taking risks for fear of rejection. I suppose it is normal to be an adolescent keenly aware of peer approval, but it is so painful to relive it in your mind's eye while watching your kiddos make similar choices. No matter how much we've encouraged, pleaded, and bribed (yes, we've stooped that low), we've not been able to push our kiddos out of a similar mind-set. Can you relate?

The thing is, you might think I'm talking about trying out for a sports team or running for a leadership position. Those are risk-taking opportunities, for sure. But when I look closely at this particular verse, I'm keenly aware that sharing the good news can become an approval battleground for all of us.

The temptation to please people becomes an obstacle in sharing the gospel, unless we remember that we are already approved messengers of God.

In every place we go, every opportunity we embrace, we are messengers approved by God. It is a calling entrusted to all of us as children of

God—and one we'll each go about in a different way. We are messengers who get to give God all the glory in the wins and losses, triumphs and failures. But first we have to move past the fear of rejection, criticism, and potential failure, as we consider the real stakes. For every time we stay silent, we're forsaking the message that's been entrusted to us to share—the good news of Jesus Christ desperately needed by a hurting world.

READ

1 Thessalonians 2:1-16

RESPOND

God, I speak as Your messenger, approved by You and entrusted with the good news. May my purpose be to please You alone, and not people. Examine the motives of my heart, God, and may You find them pure. Please forgive me for being consumed by the approval of man. Please move me into message-bearing opportunities with holy boldness for Your kingdom purposes. In Jesus' name, amen.

REFLECT

How is God calling you to embrace the call to be a message bearer approved by God who is entrusted to share the good news, and no longer consumed by seeking the approval of people?

57

This Is Real Love

This is real love—not that we loved God, but that he loved us and sent his Son as a sacrifice to take away our sins. Dear friends, since God loved us that much, we surely ought to love each other.

1 JOHN 4:10-11

Have you ever thought what real love looks like? In our English language, we use the word *love* to describe everyone and everything we are in "love, like, and lust" with. We love chocolate ice cream. We love afternoon tea and biscotti. We love Netflix and Target. The truth is that our love for these things and places is most certainly a different kind of love than what we have for our God and what He has for us and the people He's placed in our lives.

The Bible actually makes the distinction between the kinds of love we experience using three different Greek words: *eros*, *agape*, and *philos*. *Eros* is a kind of romantic love, *agape* is a kind of benevolent love, and *philos* is considered brotherly love. *Agape* is actually the word the apostle John used in the passage above as well as in the instructions we find penned by Paul in 1 Corinthians 13.[9] In Paul's case, he took a seldom-used term and infused a fresh definition of biblical love by illustrating what love looks like in action rather than feeling. He emphasized that biblical love is about giving and selflessness, not feeling and emotion, and he pointed to the source of love, God Himself, as well as our access to His love through Jesus Christ.[10]

The kind of love that comes from God isn't self-serving or consuming—it is completely and utterly sacrificial.

When God demonstrated His love for us by sacrificing His Son on our behalf to take away our sins, He showed us true love. It's a love that changes lives. It's a love that gives hope. It's a love that we are to first experience and then express as we lay down our needs, desires, and even our lives to show love one to another. That's real love.

READ

1 John 4:7-21

RESPOND

God, I believe real love is Your love, demonstrated by sending Your Son as a sacrifice to take away our sins. Please enable me to love others because of Your love for me. Forgive me when I shut down Your love. Forgive me when I'm too stingy with my time to love others sacrificially. Please give me the courage to love others authentically out of an overflow of loving You. In Jesus' name, amen.

REFLECT

How does the real love of God challenge and inspire you to think more carefully about the ways you can love others authentically and sacrificially?

58

Inner Soul Strength

I pray that from his glorious, unlimited resources he will empower you with inner strength through his Spirit.

EPHESIANS 3:16

What do you think it means to live from Christ's glorious, unlimited resources, empowered with inner strength through the Spirit? Can you imagine how God's strength flowing through you might change the way you respond to situations, navigate crisis moments, and engage with difficult people?

Not long after my oldest daughter got her license, she made a poor decision that resulted in a little "situation" in our driveway. It's an incident we talk about often (and rest assured, she's given me permission to share it with you) because of the lessons we both learned. The potential of what could have been haunted us for months. See, it wasn't her lack of skill or responsibility that was the problem. It was her inability to handle her emotions. She was flustered and frustrated, triggered by the antics of her sister and overwhelmed with all things normal for a high school senior.

Our sweet girl failed to manage her emotions in the moment because she'd yet to realize what it meant to cling to the One who could. Isn't that often the case? How many times do we get ourselves into a mess because we forget that God's got this? "Jesus Take the Wheel" may be a song, but it's a pretty good visual for what God offers us!

We need soul strength, as in the kind of power that comes from the glorious, unlimited resources of God through the working of the Holy Spirit.

Leaning into God's strength and power isn't something we learn to do in a crisis moment. It's something we have to prepare for. In the same way we have to train for a marathon (not that I'd ever do such a crazy thing), we have to daily discipline ourselves to spend time with God. We have to quiet our hearts before Him, dig deeper into the Scriptures, and invite the Holy Spirit to teach us so we can cultivate soul strength for every kind of situation in which we need God to stabilize our emotions and guide our actions.

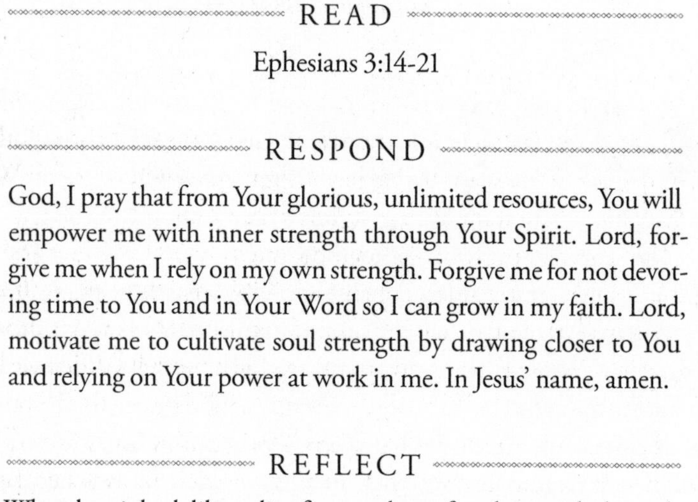

READ

Ephesians 3:14-21

RESPOND

God, I pray that from Your glorious, unlimited resources, You will empower me with inner strength through Your Spirit. Lord, forgive me when I rely on my own strength. Forgive me for not devoting time to You and in Your Word so I can grow in my faith. Lord, motivate me to cultivate soul strength by drawing closer to You and relying on Your power at work in me. In Jesus' name, amen.

REFLECT

What does it look like to live from a place of soul strength through depending on the power of God at work in you?

59

Story Hearts

Clearly, you are a letter from Christ showing the result of our ministry among you. This "letter" is written not with pen and ink, but with the Spirit of the living God. It is carved not on tablets of stone, but on human hearts.

2 CORINTHIANS 3:3

Have you ever thought of yourself as a letter from Christ for others to read? What story has He has written on your heart so far? What story do you want Him to write in the future?

The Lord had me thinking on these questions as I was preparing to speak at a women's retreat on the topic of biblical mentoring. Although I'd spoken on that topic before, this time was different as I felt a prompting from the Lord to share my testimony, even though I didn't see how it tied together.

So I started at the beginning and relayed the time I met Mrs. C that summer afternoon. I was overwhelmed by her love for Jesus and incredible faith in face of a horrific cancer battle. She made me take notice of what a life lived in the presence of God, even during a trial, could look like. That visual stuck with me as I ventured to London just a few weeks later.

Less than two months passed before I heard that Mrs. C had come face-to-face with her Savior, and that news trigger my salvation moment.

When God is about the business of writing a story on our hearts, He'll use life and death, blessings and trials, for His glory and kingdom purposes.

As I shared my story at the retreat, I wasn't the only one who couldn't hold back the tears. I noticed a woman to the left of the room visibly upset. Moments after I finished speaking, she came up to me and asked,

"What did you say was the name of that woman?" Before her name was off my lips, she explained that Mrs. C's daughter was her roommate in college more than 20 years ago, and that her own story was equally influenced for the glory of God.

Under great hardship, Mrs. C's wholehearted commitment to Jesus became her ultimate testimony. That's why the Lord wanted me to share her story within my story—to demonstrate how simple but impactful mentoring can be when it is rooted in following Christ distinctly. Her testimony became her legacy, interwoven now with mine and countless other people's. Can you imagine how God might be accomplishing a greater purpose in writing your story for His glory?

READ

2 Corinthians 3:1-18

RESPOND

God, I believe I am a letter from Christ showing the result of Your work in me—a letter written not with pen and ink, but with Your Spirit carved on my heart. Please continue to work in my life with an eternally bent purpose. May I be a living testimony leaving a lasting legacy for Your glory. In Jesus' name, amen.

REFLECT

How can you yield to the story God is writing on your heart for His glory, especially considering how He may multiply the kingdom of God through you?

Head on over to http://www.unblindedfaith.com/story/ to download the "Tell Your Story" resource as a way of remembering God's faithfulness to you and also becoming more confident in being able to share the Good News.

60

For Such a Time

And who knows but that you have come to your royal position for such a time as this?

ESTHER 4:14 NIV

Have you ever felt as if God has called you to a particular position or opportunity "for such a time as this"? I ask only because I've noticed how often this verse from Esther is quoted, but I find it interesting how the word *royal* is often left out. It's made me wonder, are we misquoting Scripture by claiming the promise for ourselves?

As you might know, Esther was a prisoner in her own land, fulfilling a divinely orchestrated plan to rescue her people by pleading on their behalf to the king. She must have been scared stiff, yet bold and courageous as she heeded her uncle's urging to take hold of her royal position for such a time as this—a time of grave danger. It's safe to say that neither you nor I have been in a royal position or expected to risk life and limb to save our people. However, if we take a moment to consider this story from a spiritual perspective, we see a few profound parallels.

We are divinely appointed by God to take up our "royal position" as servants of King Jesus "for such a time as this" in the great rescue of His lost children.

We become a part of this mission when we accept our adoption into His family by faith in Jesus Christ (Ephesians 1:11-14; 1 Peter 2:9). As heirs of Christ, we also become kingdom ambassadors and will find ourselves in the middle of a spiritual war, experiencing the Enemy's fiery darts as we do battle with the forces of evil (2 Corinthians 5:20; Ephesians 6:19-20). So you could say, as Esther did, we must put on our bravery and remember our position as we face persecution for being obedient messengers of God.

READ

Esther 4:1-17

RESPOND

God, I believe I have come to this royal position for such a time as this, which has been orchestrated for Your kingdom purposes. Please forgive me for the times I shy away from speaking boldly about You. Give me the courage to share the gospel with those who desperately need Your hope and love. In Jesus' name, amen.

REFLECT

How is God calling you to take up your royal position as a kingdom ambassador for such a time as this?

61

Do Not Fear

Do not fear, for I am with you; do not be dismayed, for I am your God. I will strengthen you and help you; I will uphold you with my righteous right hand.

ISAIAH 41:10 NIV

Do you spend more hours a day afraid than living with courageous faith? What if you leaned into the Lord with your fear, trusting Him to strengthen you, help you, and uphold you with His righteous right hand?

As I've mentioned, fear has chased me down my whole life. Of course, you'd never know, since it goes by other names—caution, prudence, and carefulness. While those are good things, they mask the real issue at hand, like the fear of getting hurt, being rejected, failing publicly, being misunderstood, or facing a devastating diagnosis. It may seem that the simplest solution for tackling these kinds of fears is to simply stop being afraid, but the reality is, putting a cease-and-desist order on our fears doesn't work.

Overcoming fear isn't about thinking less about the things that make us afraid. It's about thinking more upon the promises of God, who declares there is no need to live in fear.

Friend, it's time we walk in a faith greater than any fear. So instead of recounting our fears the next time we find ourselves afraid, why not choose to trust God more boldly by proclaiming the truth about His ability to fully uphold us in any and every situation?

READ

Isaiah 41:8-20

RESPOND

God, I will not fear, for You are with me and will strengthen me, help me, and uphold me by Your strong right hand. Forgive me for not trusting in You and Your provision. Help me believe in the promises found in Your Word and in Your faithfulness. In Jesus' name, amen.

REFLECT

How can you move beyond fear to walk in courageous faith, embracing God's promises that He will strengthen you, help you, and uphold you?

62

Heart-Centered Hospitality

Offer hospitality to one another without grumbling.

1 PETER 4:9 NIV

Are you the kind of person who is eager to share your home and go the extra mile to make your space, place, or event hospitable? Or does the idea of hospitality bring on an insatiable need to grumble?

It makes me chuckle out loud every time someone thanks me for my hospitality. Who, me? Hospitable? Nah, you're talking to the wrong person. If it were up to me, I'm sure I wouldn't open my home so easily or throw a party when the guest list size knows no limits.But see, God gave me this quiet, reserved, humble man as a husband, who happens to delight in seeing people gather together. He may not be comfortable with small talk, but he loves setting the stage for others to connect.

I'm not at all like my husband, which is probably why we're such a good match. I may be able to set a Pinterest-worthy table and arrange a guest room in a pinch, but that doesn't mean I have a heart for hospitality. But, through more than two decades of being married to a hospitality guru, I've learned a thing or two about how to open my home without stressing out or grumbling.

> Heart-centered hospitality requires making people more important than things and remembering that relationships matter more than the setting.

Yes, there is definitely something powerful about taking the time to create an inviting, comfortable space for connecting with the heart and soul of a person. It's the attention to detail—like a tablecloth and simple flower as a centerpiece—that says, "Come, sit; we've prepared a place for you." But if we only set the table for our guest and don't show up with our full attention, we're missing the heartbeat of biblical hospitality.

God wants to use us in a way that others can see Him, hear Him, and know Him personally.

For that to happen, we need to ask the Lord to give us greater visual acuity, spiritual sensitivity, and willingness to show up and be used however He sees fit. It's not about having the gift of hospitality, but rather overflowing His hospitality through our hands, feet, and mouth as ambassadors of Christ's love and grace, mercy and kindness.

READ

1 Peter 4:1-11

RESPOND

God, I will offer hospitality without grumbling. Forgive me for the times I've been caught up in excuses and given in to my own selfishness. Break me free from my insecurities and hang-ups, so I may embrace the opportunities You present me with to show hospitality to others. In Jesus' name, amen.

REFLECT

Do you have to let go of your preconceived notions about hospitality so you can embrace the call to serve others without grumbling?

63

Beckoning Onward

I'm not saying that I have this all together, that I have it made. But I am well on my way, reaching out for Christ, who has so wondrously reached out for me. Friends, don't get me wrong: By no means do I count myself an expert in all of this, but I've got my eye on the goal, where God is beckoning us onward—to Jesus. I'm off and running, and I'm not turning back.

PHILIPPIANS 3:12-14 MSG

Can you relate to Paul in admitting that he doesn't have it all together? I love how he models for us the balance of humility and holy boldness. He's a hot mess but not giving up. Because he's pressing on and reaching for Christ, remembering that Christ first reached for us. Can I hear an "Amen!"?

Through his example, Paul reminds us to steady our focus on the goal, where God is beckoning us onward to Jesus. Can you picture him in an actual race, like the opening scene from *Chariots of Fire*? Is Paul somewhere in the pack, running forward and not turning back?

One season, I made an attempt to become a runner, motivated by the track located outside my back door. Yes, it beckoned me. Slowly, I began to jog the straights, with plans to add in the turns over time. But this crazy thing happened...I discovered I loved to sprint through the turns. Forget long-distance running—I was made to run short distances, and run fast! Ironically, that totally describes my personality. Endurance over the long haul is not my strong suit. Is it yours?

In this spiritual journey, it's the long race we need to condition ourselves for as we keep pressing on.

We need to know where we are going, envisioning the prize so we can harness the motivation to run the race hard. Looking ahead matters more than considering what we've left behind. Yes, the past is worth reflecting upon to consider what was, what didn't work, what needs to still be healed. But we also need to fix our gaze ahead so we don't lose our speed and focus. So, friend, head up and lock your gaze on Jesus. Then run for the heavenly prize set aside for you to claim in Christ Jesus.

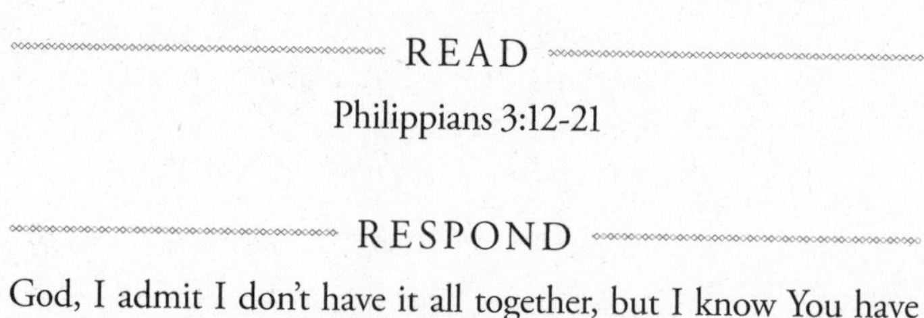

READ

Philippians 3:12-21

RESPOND

God, I admit I don't have it all together, but I know You have me on my way, reaching out for Christ who has so wondrously reached out for me. Lord, I will set my eye on the goal, where You are beckoning me onward. May I run hard and not turn back. God, if there is anything from my past holding me back, give me the courage to tend to it with You and unload the junk, so that I may run fast and free. In Jesus' name, amen.

REFLECT

Where do you find yourself today in running the race of your faith? What will it take to focus on pressing on to win the prize set aside for you in Christ?

64

The Blessing of Submission

Submit to one another out of reverence for Christ.

EPHESIANS 5:21 NIV

When you hear the word submission, does it make your stomach churn? Do you want to run for the hills? Put up a fight? Or settle into the blessing God has in store?

As a strong-willed and occasionally rebellious spirit, I've not been keen on submission. I simply don't want to be told what to do, which is what I thought submission was all about. Friend, submission isn't a dirty word when it is what you choose to give out of reverence for Christ.

In making the decision together with my husband to live and work at the boarding school right after we got married, I knew had to give up my dreams for a house with a white picket fence and a normal family schedule. But I didn't realize I was also "submitting" to having my life set in motion without consideration of my preferences. I never thought about the burden of making it to the dining hall before the bell rang for dinner, even if it meant waking up my overtired children from their naps. I didn't consider how much the "issues" in our school-owned home would bug me, especially because I couldn't fix them. Maybe this doesn't sound too different from a normal job or from renting an apartment, but there's something about the "golden handcuffs" when your friends and coworkers, home and workplace all fall under one roof.

How I longed for the institution to conform to my desires and needs. Isn't that what we all want—for the institutions over us and the people we're in relationship with to give us our way? But often it is in the limitations that we grow in humility and gratitude, and that is actually the blessing as we come to appreciate what we've been given.

If we are willing to embrace the call to biblical submission, we'll uncover the most precious gifts hidden in the very places God hems us in.

At the boarding school, there were challenges (aren't there everywhere), but when I learned to submit, I discovered the gifts I couldn't previously see. I came to appreciate the value of always having a meal provided. I learned that our earthly dwellings are temporary and to not waste time fussing over them. I discovered how rich it is to have a built-in community of friends and mentors. Most of all, I learned that submitting out of reverence for Christ really does turn a dirty word into the most beautiful blessing.

READ

Ephesians 5:1-33

RESPOND

God, I will take on a posture of submission out of reverence for Christ. Forgive me when I complain and rebel against what You've put in place for my best. Help me to see how to walk in biblical submission as part of Your good plan for my life. May I yield to Your Word and walk in humility with gratitude in the situations and relationships in which You require a posture of submission. In Jesus' name, amen.

REFLECT

How have you approached submitting to others out of reverence for Christ? How might you consider the potential blessings of obedience to God in this matter of submission.

65

Chosen and Called

You are a chosen people. You are royal priests, a holy nation, God's very own possession. As a result, you can show others the goodness of God, for he called you out of the darkness into his wonderful light.

1 PETER 2:9

How would you live differently if you believed you were chosen by God, part of a royal lineage and holy nation, God's very own possession? With that kind of identity, would you be motivated to show others the goodness of God, pointing to the ways He called you out of the darkness and into His wonderful light?

As I work with my coaching clients who are on a journey of transformation and seeking to fulfill their God-given purpose, I've witnessed how critical it is to have a foundation rooted in a biblical identity in Christ. As women, the way to put ourselves out there and use the gifts and talents God has given us rests fully upon what we believe about who we are and whose we are.

When we believe we are chosen as God's very own possession, everything about our life's purpose changes.

It's like accepting an invitation to step across a dividing line—moving from the darkness and into His marvelous light. Moving from the life we've lived apart from Christ and into the life we find in Christ. Our focus no longer becomes about our own agendas, but rather about God's divine appointments. We can boldly take risks to serve, share, lead, and influence lives, without fear of what we might lose, because our identity in Christ is secure as His very own possession (Ephesians 1:11,14 NIV). Whether our salvation story depicts God's great rescue or steady hand of faithfulness, we all belong to Him through faith in Jesus and are appointed to declare the goodness of God to everyone.

READ

1 Peter 2:4-12

RESPOND

God, I believe I am chosen by You, part of a royal and holy lineage through my adoption into Your family through faith in Christ, and Your very own possession. God, enable me to show Your goodness, as You have called me out of darkness and into Your wonderful light. Help me put on my identity in Christ. Give me a confidence in You, so that I can live from the overflow of Your work in me for the sake of Your kingdom purposes. In Jesus' name, amen.

REFLECT

What will it take to embrace your identity as His chosen child and special possession? How can you go forth declaring the goodness of God, who has called you out of darkness and into His wonderful light?

66

Enter into Rest

There is a special rest still waiting for the people of God. For all who have entered into God's rest have rested from their labors, just as God did after creating the world.

HEBREWS 4:9-10

What do you think special rest for the people of God looks like? Do you feel God expects you to rest from your labors, just as He did after creating the world?

I confess, embracing the kind of rest God offers isn't something I easily agree to. I can be pretty hardheaded and bring upon myself quite the headache. No pun intended in this case. *Ahem, confession time.* My emotional reserves were drained, and I knew full well I ought to pull back and simply rest that Sunday afternoon, especially after back-to-back speaking engagements, the fury of spring sports seasons, and preparing for my daughter's graduation party. But instead, I pressed on, pulling the weeds, planting flowers, and barking orders about the chores to the kiddos.

I refused to do what was best in heeding the Holy Spirit's prompting and my family's urging to go take a nap. I even rationalized that running a quick errand was rest, and got right back to the yard work when I returned home. Grabbing the new cast iron shepherd's hook for hanging the flower basket, I exerted all my energy attempting to shove it into the ground between the stones. Only instead of going deeper, it pivoted around and whipped me in the forehead, causing me to collapse to the ground in tears. I was certain my skull was fractured in two.

God invites and commands us to enter into rest, but it's up to us to submit and receive this gift.

Unfortunately, I had to get knocked out by the shepherd's hook to learn this truth and finally submit to rest I desperately needed. Yes, I'm a stubborn soul! I pray you learn from my painful mistake. When we refuse to obey God, we will indeed experience the consequences. When we say "no" to rest, we're saying "yes" to forgoing the kind of soul-filling refreshment we must have. But when we let go of our agenda, as we place our trust in God and His commands, we position ourselves to receive His blessing to the fullest.

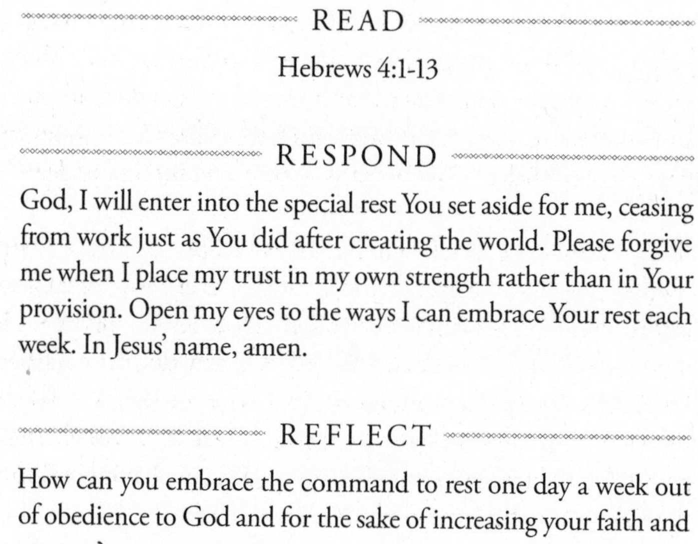

READ

Hebrews 4:1-13

RESPOND

God, I will enter into the special rest You set aside for me, ceasing from work just as You did after creating the world. Please forgive me when I place my trust in my own strength rather than in Your provision. Open my eyes to the ways I can embrace Your rest each week. In Jesus' name, amen.

REFLECT

How can you embrace the command to rest one day a week out of obedience to God and for the sake of increasing your faith and reserves?

67

Never Failing

The word of God will never fail.

LUKE 1:37

Do you really believe the Word of God will never fail? I imagine it's one of those truths most of us tend to skirt around. There's really no way we can prove that it would or wouldn't fail, so we just move on. Sure, sure, God promises *this* and *that*, but does He really intend us to believe His Word as if it were a promise made to us personally?

I think we hesitate to take God at His word because we see Him through the lens of our earthly relationships. Haven't we experienced friendships where promises were broken? How about marriages in which a spouse failed to remain faithful? Or at work, when a boss neglected his promise of a promotion? Or maybe you're guilty, as I am, of failing to keep a commitment. We've been failed. And we fail. That's just part of life lived on this earth. But we can find great hope and comfort in the promise that God's Word will never fail.

The Word of God is true always
because God is always true.

The Bible is God's love letter to us, written to guide our choices, order our thoughts, dictate our behaviors, and bring about the kind of peace, joy, and hope we long to experience. I'm sure it was hard for Mary to take into her mind and heart the proclamation that "the Word of God will never fail." Yet she responded with such great faith, declaring "I am the Lord's servant. May everything you have said about me come true" (Luke 1:8). So shall we follow Mary's lead and build our lives on the truth that the Word will never fail?

READ

Luke 1:26-38

RESPOND

God, I choose to believe Your Word will never fail. Help me to live according to Your truth, as it is found in Your Word, with unwavering certainty and unquenchable faith. In Jesus' name, amen.

REFLECT

How is the Lord inviting you to believe His Word is true and will never fail?

68

Your True Treasure

Wherever your treasure is, there the desires of your heart will also be.

MATTHEW 6:21

What do you count as a treasure? If you were to evaluate how you use your time and money, would that be an accurate assessment of your treasures and where your heart is?

Maybe it's time for a treasure inventory? Because the reality is, most of us are sinking our resources into things moths will eat, rust will rot, and thieves will break in and steal (Matthew 6:19-20). Our earthly treasures are busy stealing our time, attention, and dollars, while causing us to forsake God-appointed opportunities to store up our treasures in heaven—treasures that will be there for us when we meet our Maker face-to-face. What do those treasures look like? Our treasures ought to be people God saves by the blood of Jesus as He uses us in His kingdom work.

We are not the ones who go about saving souls, but we are Christ's ambassadors commissioned to be His hands and feet and mouthpieces on this earth.

So what does it look like to shift our efforts into investing in the kingdom treasury of souls saved for eternity? How can our time and resources be focused on loving and serving the people God places in our lives rather than being consumed by our things, comforts, and personal gains?

Yes, we have to go to work—out of the home and in it, paid and unpaid, titled and untitled—but the question is, in what manner will we do so? Will it be as an undercover agent of the Lord, prepared to spread His love in tangible ways? Or will we push God aside so we can focus on making more money to pay for another home décor item? Will we work toward that next big promotion just to get more kudos and cash or to expand our sphere of influence for the kingdom of God?

There will always be a balance between filling the spaces and time we have with the things that bring us delight (and maybe are practical too) while remembering that it is the heart of God for His people and His kingdom in which our treasures should be found.

READ

Matthew 6:19-34

RESPOND

God, I believe wherever my treasure is, there the desires of my heart will also be. Please forgive me, Lord, for the times I am not careful to consider the hold my worldly treasures have upon me. Convict me when the desires of my heart no longer line up with the desires You have for me. In Jesus' name, amen.

REFLECT

How are the desires of your heart evidenced by the things you treasure with your time, money, and attention?

69

Blessed Is the One

Blessed is the one who does not walk in step with the wicked or stand in the way that sinners take or sit in the company of mockers, but whose delight is in the law of the Lord, and who meditates on his law day and night. That person is like a tree planted by streams of water, which yields its fruit in season and whose leaf does not wither—whatever they do prospers.

PSALM 1:1-3 NIV

Does the promise of being blessed capture your attention in this verse? It does for me! But look at that long list of what it takes to be blessed: We have to avoid walking in step with the wicked, standing in the way of sinners, and sitting in the company of mockers. Isn't it interesting how nearly every posture is described—walking, standing, and sitting? Looks like we need to be aware of what we're doing all the time! The psalmist also reminds us where to set our continual focus—delighting in the law of the Lord, meditating on His law day and night. God brings spiritual growth and sustainability through a steady feeding of Scripture.

Whether we're walking, standing, sitting, sleeping, or daydreaming, the Word is to be on our mind.

The psalmist also urges us to plant ourselves down by streams of water. Not literally, of course. (Although I'd love to turn this verse into a requirement to have a house by the shore or lake or even a little pond.) Back to reality—we need to carefully plant ourselves in an environment designed for cultivating growth. Just like a plant, the sustainability of our faith, along with the blessings we hope to receive from the Lord, is directly linked to where we put down our roots, the ways we go about feeding our soul, and the careful considering of what elements we're exposed to, including the measure of *Sonlight* we receive on a daily basis.

As I've mentioned before, this area of plant growth isn't exactly my specialty. I've witnessed such demise in my precious little succulents as I neglect their care and then panic, overwater, and watch as they die an awful drowning death. Isn't the same true about our spiritual life? Are we setting ourselves up to thrive or simply survive in light of whom we're walking this journey of faith with, in what circles of influences we're sitting, and how much time we're devoting to being in the Word?

READ

Psalm 1:1-6

RESPOND

God, I believe I must not walk in step with the wicked, stand in the way sinners take, or sit in the company of mockers, but I should delight in Your law and meditate on it day and night, so I may be like a tree planted by streams of water, which yields its fruit in season and whose leaf does not wither—whatever I do may prosper. Lord, forgive me when I go elsewhere for nourishment. Keep me from neglecting time with You and in the Word. May I tend to cultivating spiritual roots, carefully and purposefully considering the people and places and agendas influencing my faith journey. In Jesus' name, amen.

REFLECT

Where are you planted, how are you being nurtured, and how are you growing in your faith?

Head on over to http://www.unblindedfaith/com/influence/ to download the Life Influence worksheet to help you prayerfully connect with God and look for ways to carve out time to be in the Word and fellowship with other believers.

70

Give Your Burdens

Give your burdens to the Lord, and he will take care of you. He will not permit the godly to slip and fall.

PSALM 55:22

What does it look like for you to give your burdens to the Lord, trusting that He will take care of you? Do you believe He will not permit you to slip and fall when you pursue living His way?

I think I have an idea of what it looks like to carry burdens far greater than we were intended to strap upon our backs, thanks to the time I was in college and backpacked from England to France. It never occurred to me that the heavier the bag to lift, the heavier the load to carry…for the whole journey. Our first day included traveling by train, boat, subway, and a whole lot of hoofing it around Paris to see the sights, all with my backpack on. I was exhausted by the time we crashed on the floor of a friend's hotel room (ah, poor college kids trying to save money), and I woke up feeling as if I'd been hit by a tractor trailer.

As we set out for another day, I knew my weary body was done but ignored the warning signs and pressed on. That evening, as we gathered with friends at the Eiffel Tower, I attempted to sit on a pillar I thought was made of cement to give my feet and back a rest, but it turned out to be rubber. When it buckled under me, I collapsed to the ground, dislocating my knee for the umpteenth time. My friends carried me to the police station located nearby, and I was swiftly taken to the hospital by ambulance. Not exactly how I hoped to see Paris. Hours later, I was discharged with an unstable knee wrapped in an Ace bandage and medical tape. It was a disaster!

> How often do we insist on carrying an emotional and spiritual burden that is greater than what we can humanly handle, all while Jesus stands before us and offers to carry it for us?

What was my burden the day before became even greater with my injury, until one of my two travel mates did the most Christlike thing imaginable. She carried my bag along with hers. She didn't ask me to unload it to make it lighter. She didn't mock me for overpacking. She simply took my load and carried it for me. Isn't that all Jesus wants to do for us?

READ

Psalm 55:1-23

RESPOND

God, I believe I can give my burdens to You, and You will take care of me, keeping me from slipping and falling. May I trust my burdens to You. Please carry the load I was never meant to bear. Thank You for being the One I can lean on always. In the strong name of Jesus, amen.

REFLECT

How has Jesus stepped in to carry your load? What burden is He ready to carry for you that you need to release to Him?

71

Cast Your Cares

Cast all your anxiety on him because he cares for you.

1 PETER 5:7 NIV

Are you in the habit of casting all your anxiety on the Lord? How does the promise that He cares for you inspire you to trust Him more?

Friend, He careth for you. Let that soak in, even though I know it sounds funny. But that's exactly how I memorized this verse from the King James version, thanks to a little plaque belonging to my husband's grandfather, which hung over my kitchen sink for years. As I washed dishes night after night, thinking about Grandpa Ferdinand, who lost his wife to cancer and raised their two girls on his own, I asked God to make me into a woman who would quickly cast "all my care upon him; for he careth for [me]."

As life marched on fast and furiously, I found it hard and harder to believe this truth. I worried about our financial stability with our mounting expenses. I was fearful of cancer becoming a bigger part of our story. I was anxious about the impact of my parenting on the kiddos, in light of some of the junk I was still working through. I was so busy trying to solve the problems in my head that I was actually growing more and more anxious. Can you relate?

God knows our worries can easily turn into anxiety, which is why He tells us to cast our cares on Him.

The problem is that our anxious thoughts aren't so simple to work through. At times we need the help of a professional Christian counselor, whom God can use to bring healing and relief from the kind of debilitating anxiety that is both real and highly treatable. God is for us.

He wants to carry our cares to the cross and keep them there. So shall we let Him any way He sees fit?

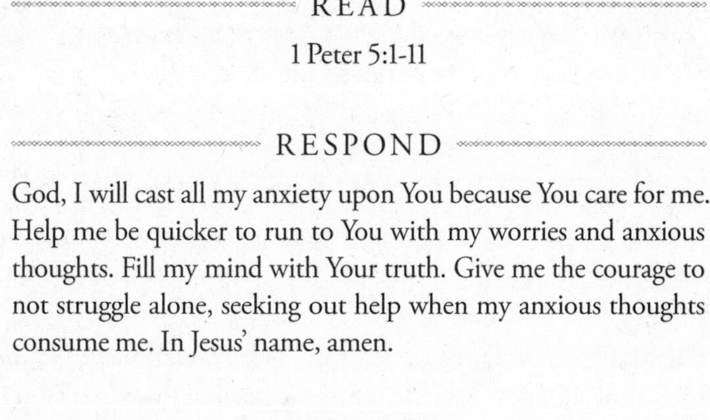

READ

1 Peter 5:1-11

RESPOND

God, I will cast all my anxiety upon You because You care for me. Help me be quicker to run to You with my worries and anxious thoughts. Fill my mind with Your truth. Give me the courage to not struggle alone, seeking out help when my anxious thoughts consume me. In Jesus' name, amen.

REFLECT

How can you be motivated to cast your cares upon God by considering God's faithfulness in caring for you?

72

Suffering Our Share

We are pressed on every side by troubles, but we are not crushed. We are perplexed, but not driven to despair. We are hunted down, but never abandoned by God. We get knocked down, but we are not destroyed. Through suffering, our bodies continue to share in the death of Jesus so that the life of Jesus may also be seen in our bodies.

2 CORINTHIANS 4:8-11

Have you felt pressed in on every side by trouble? Crushed and perplexed? Hunted down and knocked down? Well then, you're well acquainted with suffering. My guess is that in the face of suffering, you did your best to run from it, deflect it, blame it, and hide from it. Isn't that our normal response? We don't like pain, but we can't avoid it forever.

I once heard a pastor say, "We're either in the middle of a trial, coming through a trial, or about to head into one." Oh, great; there's happy news. But if suffering is a part of life, why not figure out how to suffer well? Instead of denying its reality, how about preparing for it now? For example, I know from past experiences that I'll be sure to feel pressed in and knocked down at key times—like when I'm preparing to speak, writing a book, or seeking to serve others in a practical way. But because the trial is so predictable, I can prepare in advance by spending time steeped in Scripture and seeking prayer support, while being wise to leave emotional reserves for the spiritual battle ahead.

We don't have to face suffering with a defeated mindset when we remember our victory is found in the cross.

God promises us that when we suffer, we share in the suffering of Christ—the One who overcame death on our behalf. Yes, He was pressed in, but not crushed. He was perplexed, but not driven to despair. He was hunted down, but never abandoned. He was knocked down, but not destroyed. He suffered. And we suffer. But He rose again, victorious. And in Christ, so will we.

READ

2 Corinthians 4:1-16

RESPOND

God, I believe I will be pressed on every side by trouble, but not crushed; perplexed but not driven to despair; hunted down but not abandoned by You; knocked down, but not destroyed—and through suffering like this, I will experience a share in the death of Jesus so the life of Jesus may be seen by others. God, thank You for giving me the Word to help me understand the ways I'll suffer and how to persevere. May I have the courage to share in the suffering of Christ for the sake of a testimony that gives You glory. In Jesus' name, amen.

REFLECT

What would it look like to prepare in advance to suffer well and to lean on the body of Christ when suffering comes upon you?

73

Build Each Other Up

Encourage each other and build each other up, just as you are already doing.

1 THESSALONIANS 5:11

As you think back upon your life, maybe even focusing on just your childhood, can you pinpoint times you were truly encouraged and built up by those you were doing life with? Has one particular person spurred you on to be all that God intended? Have you been this person in someone else's life?

God designed us to be His hands and feet as we seek authentic ways to encourage one another and build each other up in word and deed, by example and by faith.

And yet, as His children, we often think our influence doesn't matter all that much. How wrong we are! Sometimes the difference we make will never be known, but it can entirely change the course of someone's life. Like my childhood friend Jen. She was kind and gentle. Funny and awkward. Humble and apologetic to a fault. Honestly, she was such a Goody-Two-Shoes, I pulled back from our friendship during our high school years because I was too afraid of disappointing her with my rebellious antics. So foolish!

When I returned home from that semester in London as a Christian, Jen was one of the first people I told about my newfound faith. I'll never forget her affirming words: "The best thing that has ever happened to you was finding God in London." Seeing as Jen was Jewish, her encouragement definitely took me by surprise. If only I had urged her to see Yeshuvah as the Messiah before cancer stole her life two decades later.

As I think of her legacy, I'm challenged to consider mine ever more closely, especially as I represent Christ through the testimony of my faith. Jen never missed an opportunity to affirm my value. Am I doing the same for others? She was a pure-hearted encourager. Am I seeking to encourage others with the hope of Christ? She nudged me toward the leading of God. Would others say that is what I am doing too?

READ

1 Thessalonians 5:1-11

RESPOND

God, I will make time to encourage and build up those You've placed in my life. Please challenge me to consider the example I'm setting by the way I live. Show me opportunities to share Your love and serve in Your name. Give me courage to step out in humble but bold faith to love others in Your name. In Jesus' name, amen.

REFLECT

How may God want you to encourage and build others up in your family, workplace, ministry, and friendships?

74

Kindness and Grace

He is so rich in kindness and grace that he purchased our freedom with the blood of his Son and forgave our sins.

EPHESIANS 1:7

Do you typically think of God as being rich in kindness? Do you see His grace manifested in the way He purchased our freedom with the blood of Jesus for the forgiveness of our sins?

Isn't it amazing how we can spend years reading the Bible and walking with the Lord, and yet there are principles and truths that we completely miss? For example, I never thought of the richness of God's kindness even though I was abundantly aware of His extravagant grace in my life. It took the continual reminders from a gal in my Bible study group to help me see the constant gift of God's kindness. As our group wrestled through the implications of heeding the Scriptures, while waiting on God's provision and moving through some truly painful circumstances, Eileen would bring us back to the truth: *God is kind. His kindness is for us.*

God is so kind, He poured out His grace for our freedom.

God is so kind, He gave his one and only Son as a sacrifice for our sins, as He purchased our lives through Jesus' shed blood. He loves us so much, He chose to shower our lives with His kindness, wisdom, and understanding (Ephesians 1:8).

So what keeps us from seeing the kindness of God daily? Is it because we think *kind* means we get what we want? What if the kindness of God were about giving us what we need eternally, even if that means we struggle while on this earth? Maybe His kindness is the reason we can experience hope and peace while we wait to meet our Maker face-to-face.

READ

Ephesians 1:3-10

RESPOND

God, I believe You are so rich in kindness and grace, You purchased my freedom with the blood of Your Son and forgave my sins. Forgive me when I don't recognize the truth You make so plain. Give me eyes to see how You manifest Your kindness in my life, so I may joyfully proclaim it to others. In Jesus' name, amen.

REFLECT

How have you seen the kindness of God manifest in your life over the last week, month, or maybe even year or lifetime? What can you do to remind yourself to be intentional about looking for His kindness going forward?

75

When We Ask

Keep on asking, and you will receive what you ask for. Keep on seeking, and you will find. Keep on knocking, and the door will be opened to you. For everyone who asks, receives. Everyone who seeks, finds. And to everyone who knocks, the door will be opened.

MATTHEW 7:7-8

What do you think God really means by urging us to keep asking Him for what we think we need or want? Does that mean anything and at any time? Honestly, this urging to keep on asking makes no sense to me. It actually feels counterintuitive to how we ought to approach our Father in heaven. Do you feel this way too?

As a parent, if my children keep badgering me for an answer, I usually react irritably and issue a firm warning: "If you ask me again, the answer will be *no*! I will make my decision when I am ready." Their persistence makes me feel as if they don't respect my authority, and I fear that a bit of entitlement, selfishness, and arrogance might be motivating their ongoing petition. But on the other hand, I do want them to come to me with everything. I want to know their desires, longings, hopes, and dreams, even if I can't fulfill them because they're not in their best interest or beneficial to the greater good. I imagine God wants that for us too.

When God invites us to ask Him for everything and anything, He doesn't turn a blind eye to the state of our hearts and His kingdom purposes.

As Sovereign God, He knows the difference between our needs and wants, the state of our hearts, and our truest motives. He knows what is in line with His perfect will. But if that is the case, why does He urge us to pursue Him with everything and anything? Well, maybe because He wants us to lay our requests before Him in order to cultivate an intimate and honest relationship with Him. At the heart of the matter, our heavenly Father wants His children to bring before Him every single desire and request, just as we want that of our children, all the while trusting that His answer is the best.

READ

Matthew 7:7-10

RESPOND

God, I will keep on asking, seeking, and knocking, so I will receive what I ask for, find what I'm looking for, and discover that open door, according to Your will. Thank You for permission to seek out Your provision and approach You with every need. Please forgive me, when I hold back and doubt Your abilities to provide and move me into full submission to Your will. In Jesus' name, amen.

REFLECT

What might change if you looked at this instruction from the perspective of cultivating a deeper relationship with God as your heavenly Father rather than as a laundry list of demands for Him to heed?

76

No Regrets

The kind of sorrow God wants us to experience leads us away from sin and results in salvation. There's no regret for that kind of sorrow. But worldly sorrow, which lacks repentance, results in spiritual death.

2 CORINTHIANS 7:10

Have you experienced the kind of sorrow that leads away from sin and results in salvation? Or do you find yourself plagued by a kind of worldly sorrow, uncertain about how to experience repentance and avoid spiritual death? I know this is quite the topic to consider, but we can't simply focus on the verses that make us feel good. We need to become honest students of Scripture, willing to wrestle through even the uncomfortable teachings—like this one distinguishing between godly sorrow and worldly sorrow.

The most challenging portions of Scripture are often the most beneficial to unpack because they address the root issue—our sin problem—and the way out. Our sin isn't the end of the story. The blood of Jesus ended that story through His forgiveness for our sins. In Him, we get to move forward into freedom, but first we have to experience the kind of regret and guilt that leads to sorrow and paves the way to repentance.

Through our honest confession of sin before God, we find the freedom from guilt our souls crave.

Does your guilt feel like a pile of bricks six feet high resting on your chest? Is there a tape playing over and over again in your head about that thing you did back then—maybe even before you realized it was wrong? Friend, that's sorrow over sin that God is poised and ready to take from you. And that's why Jesus died on the cross—to pay the price for debt you could not satisfy. So why continue to carry it rather than be set free by the blood shed by Jesus Christ?

Yes, it's actually a good thing when we feel bad about our behavior, because that's where the turnaround begins. That's when we can move toward the Lord, in humble confession, asking for His grace and forgiveness to change us from the inside out. And as we stand in His presence, covered by His love and wrapped in His mercy, the path to repentance becomes abundantly clear. Sin isn't the problem, friend. Refusing to admit our sin is the real issue keeping us from experiencing the fullness of life God offers.

READ

2 Corinthians 7:5-16

RESPOND

God, I will not run from the kind of sorrow You want me to experience that will lead me away from sin and result in salvation, because there is no regret for the kind of sorrow that fosters repentance. Please keep me from excusing my sin and move me into owning it, so I can repent and walk in full forgiveness and freedom in Christ. In Jesus' name, amen.

REFLECT

How is God inviting you to move into godly sorrow that leads to repentance?

77

The Ministry of Generosity

As a result of your ministry, they will give glory to God. For your generosity to them and to all believers will prove that you are obedient to the Good News of Christ.

2 CORINTHIANS 9:13

What is the ministry God has called you to? Or do you think to be in ministry, you have to be a missionary or at least serve at a church as a leader or pastor? If that is really the only way to be in ministry, what do we do with this verse?

If we dig into 2 Corinthians 9, we'll discover there is a kind of ministry we can all participate in—the ministry of generosity. But what exactly does that look like? Well, Paul gives us an insider's look. He describes how a farmer who plants only a few seeds will get a small crop, but the one who plants generously will get a generous crop (2 Corinthians 9:6). Actually, I understand that just a bit, as I look out my window and see a half dozen ready-to-bloom sunflowers. What a bummer that we planted only about two dozen seedpods in the ground—imagine if we had sown more seeds!

As Paul describes, we decide how many seeds to plant in the first place (2 Corinthians 9:7). In the case of our sunflowers, we planted only a few because the task seemed daunting at the time. I was reluctant to put in the effort, doubting they'd ever bloom and grow. But oh, my, I'm regretting that we didn't plant more!

We have the freedom in Christ to decide how we'll sow into kingdom work—will it be generously or reluctantly?

Goodness, we can be so stingy, even though God promises to generously provide all we need, so we will always have plenty left over to share with others (2 Corinthians 9:7-8). Embracing a ministry of generosity in our financial giving to God's kingdom work is a privilege and calling, but like everything God gives us to steward, we get to decide in our hearts how invested we want to become. It's our choice to be generous with our time, talents, and resources in obedience to the good news. Now that is quite a mission of ministry, don't you think?

READ

2 Corinthians 9:1-14

RESPOND

God, I want to invest in the kind of ministry that gives glory to You, striving for generosity toward those You've put in my life so they, and You, will see I'm obedient to share the good news of Christ. Thank You for making a place for me to serve in every setting. Move me into a ministry of generosity as I seek to use the talents, gifts, and resources You've given me for Your kingdom purposes. In Jesus' name, amen.

REFLECT

What opportunities do you see to sow into a ministry of generosity? What would change in your life if you embraced those opportunities?

78

For the Good

We know that God causes everything to work together for the good of those who love God and are called according to his purpose for them.

ROMANS 8:28

Is it hard for you to believe God causes everything to work together for the good of those who love Him and are called according to His purpose? Do you get irritated and frustrated when things don't go as planned? Do you take matters into your own hands? Or do you submit to the Lord, agreeing with His will, His way, for His glory?

Maybe you can guess my response by now. Yes, my yielding is messy and noisy. As I often say, I'm a square log you'll hear *thump, thump, thumping* along as I desperately try to roll with God's plan. It's especially loud when I find myself at a detour caused by Satan's handiwork or maybe my own misunderstanding of God's purposes. Can you relate? I'm often left wondering, did I say yes when I should have said no? Did the Enemy get a foothold in this situation?

For example, I thought I clearly heard from God when I said yes to a speaking invitation after praying about it and seeking counsel. After agreeing and announcing it on my website, the planners turned around and withdrew the offer as they felt led in another direction. I felt absolutely awful—even though the conference planner said I hadn't done anything wrong and apologized profusely.

Although it was such a minor issue in the big scheme of life, it became an open door for me to doubt God's purposes. Satan tempts us to question God's sovereignty in the big things as much as he does in the little things, striving to wear down our souls (Daniel 7:25 ESV)! Whether we're facing rejection or loss, minor disappointments or devastating news, the challenge is for us to cling to the truth. What my husband said to me in that fleeting issue applies in the major ones too: "God will accomplish everything for the good of those who love Him (Romans 8:28), so even if the Enemy did get into this situation, God will have the final say."

> Yes it is true—God works for the good of those who love Him, always and in all situations.

While my experience is only a blip on the radar screen, the character of God is the same in every situation. By faith we can choose to believe this promise from God that He is always at work, in every situation (even the ones that make us grieve and scream and sob hard), for the good of those who love Him.

READ

Romans 8:18-30

RESPOND

God, I believe You cause everything to work together for the good of those who love You and are called according to Your purpose. You are always on the throne, even when life is messy. You are still God of the universe, even when I don't know what You're doing. Please increase my faith and trust in Your good purposes. In Jesus' name, amen.

REFLECT

How can trusting in God's plans to work everything together for the good of those who love Him change how you face obstacles and detours in your life?

79

The Same But Different

There are different kinds of spiritual gifts, but the same Spirit is the source of them all. There are different kinds of service, but we serve the same Lord. God works in different ways, but it is the same God who does the work in all of us.

1 CORINTHIANS 12:4-6

Have you considered the kind of spiritual gifting God has given you, and are you actively pursuing opportunities to use that gifting for His glory?

Yes, God created within us a gift to be used for the greater good in the body of Christ.

I think one of the ways we sabotage the work of God in our lives is by fixing our eyes on what He is doing in everyone else rather than carefully and purposefully joining Him in the work He's busy accomplishing in us and through us—especially in the use of our gifts. Would you agree?

It's not about how we feel about our gifting, but rather how we receive it and use it for His glory. He chooses when and how and where to distribute the gifts to us, which are wisdom, special knowledge, faith, healing, power to perform miracles, ability to prophesy, discerning a message from the Spirit of God, speaking in tongues, and interpreting what is being said (1 Corinthians 12:7-11).

How easily we fall into the comparison trap and pit of jealousy, wanting "another" gift—or another life—instead of being grateful for the one we've been given. I often have to speak truth to my soul and remind myself, "If I want the *good* I see in her life, I also have to be willing to take on her *bad* as well." Do you need to speak this to your heart and mind too?

In every aspect of our lives there is good and bad, strength and weakness, beautiful gifting and even the lack thereof. That's because God designed the body of Christ to be completed by one another.

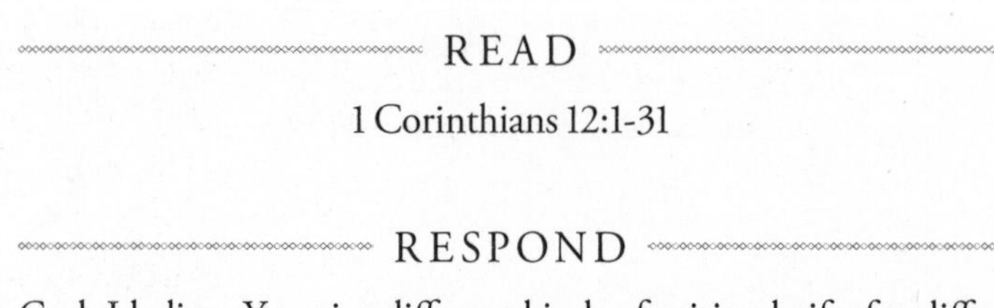

READ

1 Corinthians 12:1-31

RESPOND

God, I believe You give different kinds of spiritual gifts for different kinds of services, but You're busy working in and through me and my fellow brothers and sisters in Christ for Your glory. Please forgive me when I neglect my gifting and covet what I see in others. Please fill me with a heart of gratitude and desire to serve using the gift You've chosen for me for the sake of Your work in the body of Christ. In Jesus' name, amen.

REFLECT

Is it time to focus on using the spiritual gifting God has given you right where He has planted you? How might you do that?

Head on over to http://www.unblindedfaith.com/spiritual-gifts/ to download the Spiritual Gifts worksheet to help you prayerfully connect with God and look for ways you can serve the body of Christ.

80

Everyday Missionary

By God's grace and mighty power, I have been given the privilege of serving him by spreading this Good News.

EPHESIANS 3:7

When you think of what it means to serve God, what comes to mind? Could it be the Lord simply wants to use you, by His grace and mighty power, in one relationship at a time?

I'm not sure how or when exactly the idea of being an "everyday missionary" became a part of my thinking. Maybe it was a result of living at a boarding school and recognizing that gospel sharing can happen in any context—around the dinner table, standing on the sidelines of a football game, or traveling on a bus to a weekend retreat. I may not have had a Bible in hand, but I quickly discovered that by doing life side by side, we had an open door of opportunity to share the good news. That's because chitchat can turn into conversation, and conversation can lead to questions about Jesus and the gospel—everywhere.

We can be everyday missionaries in the most unlikely of mission fields.

Think about the places you connect with people—doctor's offices, sporting events, and volunteer opportunities. Yes, those are all mission fields. I've spent hours in treatment for my knees, hips, and back, all the while sharing the gospel with a half-dozen physical therapists who were a captive audience while working on my body. Maybe that's why God kept me injured. At least I used the time well!

Where might God use you as an everyday missionary? Your workplace? Where you serve your community? The sidelines of your kiddo's games? Maybe even standing in line at a superstore?

READ

Ephesians 3:1-7

RESPOND

God, I believe by Your grace and mighty power, I've been given the privilege of serving You by spreading this good news. Please forgive me when I ignore, avoid, or run from the opportunities You place before me. Give me courage and creativity to tell others about Jesus, as I lean in to Your grace and mighty power. In Jesus' name, amen.

REFLECT

How might God be inviting you to share the good news right where He's planted you?

81

Steady That Mind

You will keep in perfect peace those whose minds are steadfast, because they trust in you.

ISAIAH 26:3 NIV

Imagine what it would look like to experience a kind of perfect peace that comes from your mind being steady on God—steady because you trust Him entirely. Sounds lovely, right? But maybe this is a challenge because you're the type of person who can see problems before they hit. Do you anticipate which consequences will ensue? Are you worried about what will happen "if"?

A dear friend used to remind me, "Don't borrow trouble from tomorrow." That's because I can be quite good at seeing down the pike and predicting the consequences. I always want a plan B in case plan A fails. Can you relate? As a long-term thinker, it's such a challenge to stay in the moment and focus on God's faithfulness. Instead, my mind runs ahead, trying to solve the problem in advance.

If we don't steady our minds on God's truth, we can fret ourselves into a hot mess.

Is that your norm? Well, the good news is we can turn our fretting into something good by choosing instead to pray and seek God for His purposes. Instead of worrying, we can pray for those needs we anticipate, not only in our own lives but also on behalf of those God lays on our hearts. We can soak up the Word and leading of the Holy Spirit, seeking the Lord to show us the steps to take next. We can throw out the lies and fears consuming our thoughts and steady our minds on the truth, reminding ourselves who God is and how His faithfulness prevails.

Even if plan B seems worth having in our back pockets, we serve a plan-A God whose purposes far exceed our limited understanding and whose redemption is far greater than anything we can accomplish on our own.

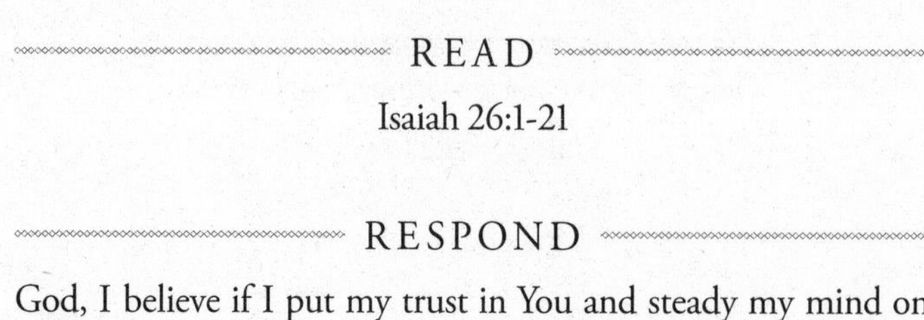

READ

Isaiah 26:1-21

RESPOND

God, I believe if I put my trust in You and steady my mind on Your truth, You will give me perfect peace. Thank You for providing a way for me to stay in the moment. Help me to turn to You and pray instead of coming up with plan B. Lord, remind me to run to Your Word for wisdom in all things and trust in Your plan A. In Jesus' name, amen.

REFLECT

What steps can you take to move from worry and "what if" to steadying your mind on the truth as you lean into the calling to pray and seek God for His wisdom?

82

Worthy Already

We keep on praying for you, asking our God to enable you to live a life worthy of his call. May he give you the power to accomplish all the good things your faith prompts you to do.

2 THESSALONIANS 1:11

What do you think it means to live a life worthy of His call? Have you settled your soul on the truth that you are indeed worthy and called? That He is at work in you, giving you the power to accomplish all the good things your faith prompts you to do?

Based on my experiences with the women I coach, I see how quickly and effectively the Enemy undermines our sense of worth, and by doing so, sabotages the calling of God. Instead of believing our worth comes from God alone, we buy the lie that our worth is based on performance, achievements, and even our social status. So we work hard, try harder, and even pick up a self-esteem chant or two, as though we just need to activate our inner cheerleader. Ah, no. Toss the pom-poms to the curb, girlfriend, because we don't need what the world calls self-esteem. When we focus on positive self-esteem, we're simply trying to boost our ego by only noticing what is awesome about ourselves. But that doesn't work because there's really nothing awesome about a sinner saved by grace, other than the grace-Giver Himself.

Our worth is secure in Christ, and our purpose is defined by God alone.

In Christ we receive our biblical identity once and for all. That identity was established by God when He made us in His image, rescued us from sin through the blood of Jesus, and adopted us as His children (Romans 5:9). The same power that raised Christ from the dead is alive and active in us by faith in Jesus Christ as Lord and through the working of the Holy Spirit. And it is this remarkable power that enables us to accomplish our calling and those things prompted by our faith (Romans 8:11; Ephesians 1:19-20).

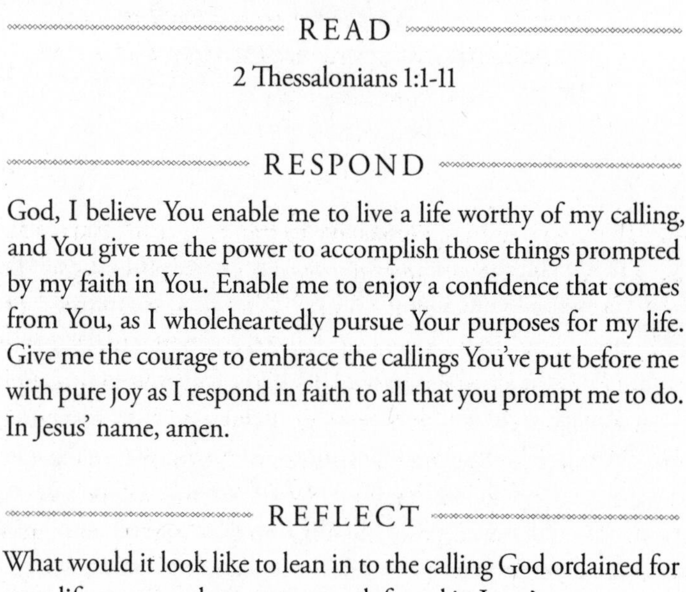

READ

2 Thessalonians 1:1-11

RESPOND

God, I believe You enable me to live a life worthy of my calling, and You give me the power to accomplish those things prompted by my faith in You. Enable me to enjoy a confidence that comes from You, as I wholeheartedly pursue Your purposes for my life. Give me the courage to embrace the callings You've put before me with pure joy as I respond in faith to all that you prompt me to do. In Jesus' name, amen.

REFLECT

What would it look like to lean in to the calling God ordained for your life as you embrace your worth found in Jesus?

83

Serving the Creator

They traded the truth about God for a lie. So they worshiped and served the things God created instead of the Creator himself, who is worthy of eternal praise! Amen.

ROMANS 1:25

What do you think it looks like to trade the truth about God for a lie? How about worshiping and serving the created things instead of the Creator Himself? Maybe you can think of this another way: Does the outcome of your efforts matter more than pleasing God by being obedient to what He has called you to accomplish?

For example, do you find yourself making a list so you can cross it off? Do you take on a project because of how it will make you feel, rather than what God has to say about it? Are you willing to compromise God's instructions about Sabbath and fellowship, rest and kindness, just to *get 'er done*?

> We need to learn how to live in the "undone" of life, because our "doings" are not greater than the One who made us to accomplish all things for His glory.

God created us to worship Him, not our work. To serve Him, not our accomplishments. To be stewards of our callings, not defined by them. To be creators made in His image, not enslaved to the creative accomplishing process.

Satan set the stage for Eve to fall into temptation and disobedience when he twisted a truth into a lie by switching around some words and leaving a few out (Genesis 3:1). It was a subtle but effective tactic—one he uses with us today—to take the good thing God has called us to and turn it with the slight tweak of a word or motive. That's why, my friends, we've got to be vigilant against the Enemy's schemes and cognizant of the motives of our hearts, so our true worship is for God alone.

READ

Romans 1:18-32

RESPOND

God, I will guard against trading a truth about You for a lie and ending up worshiping and serving my own created thing instead of You, my Creator. Lord, forgive me when I get caught up in productivity instead of Your purposes. Help me see my work and effort as a form of worship and service unto You and for Your glory, and not make it into a god. In Jesus' name, amen.

REFLECT

How do you get caught in the trap of worshiping the created thing rather than the Creator Himself?

84

Refreshment Redefined

The generous will prosper; those who refresh others will themselves be refreshed.

PROVERBS 11:25

Have you ever noticed how God takes a simple concept and turns it upside down? Through the Old and New Testament alike, we see basic life principles that require counter-cultural application. For example, how can it be that generosity will lead to prosperity? Or how can serving others lead to refreshment?

We believe we don't have enough, so we can't imagine giving anything away, because we're operating with a poverty mind-set. We think we don't have enough money because we can't take that exotic Caribbean trip. Yet, in reality, we have all we need if we can put food on the table. We hesitate to host a simple social gathering or fix the coffee at women's Bible study, but if we're spending time on social media and watching Netflix, don't we have enough hours to devote to hospitality and serving others.

I wonder if our poverty mind-set stems from a time when we really were short on funds or emotional reserves. Maybe the season of beans and rice feels all too familiar. Maybe margin space hasn't been around long enough to believe it is here to stay.

Maybe we need to let go of what we do have to receive the "more" God has in store for us.

Jesus teaches in Luke 6:38, "Give, and you will receive. Your gift will return to you in full—pressed down, shaken together to make room for more, running over, and poured into your lap. The amount you give will determine the amount you get back." We can give from the little we have, both in time and finances, following in the footsteps of the widow who gave away all she had to live on (Luke 21:1-4). She knew what we've yet to find out—that because of God's provision, we can be more and more generous as we give from the overflow of His provision.

READ

Proverbs 11:1-31

RESPOND

God, I believe You can prosper me through my generosity, and I will be refreshed when I choose to refresh others. Show me how to be even more generous today than I was yesterday. Open my eyes to see how I'm living with a poverty mind-set. Give me the courage to serve others, even out of my comfort zone, and trust You for the refreshment I crave. In Jesus' name, amen.

REFLECT

Could God be waiting for you to move toward others in seeking to serve and refresh their needs, before giving you a full measure of His generosity and refreshment?

Let It Flow

Anyone who believes in me may come and drink! For the Scriptures declare, "Rivers of living water will flow from his heart."

JOHN 7:38

Why do we refuse to go to the source of living water for the soul-filling, heart-quenching nourishment we crave? Instead, we hope others will fill our cup to the brim. But is this what God intended? Or does He present us with a radical alternative?

By faith in Jesus Christ, we get access to rivers of living water. Can you hear the sound of it rushing straight toward you? It's alive, full of energy. Flowing strong. It's not some trickling brook filled by a nearly dried-up dam. There is a river, friends—one "whose streams make glad the city of God, the holy place where the Most High dwells" (Psalm 46:4 NIV). Imagine being filled up with such a river.

What would we bring to this world if we were so filled up with Jesus that all that ever flowed out of us was more of Him?

More of Jesus, less of me. More of Jesus, less seeking out false gods in everyone and everything else. Oh, yes, we're guilty of wandering from person to person and thing to thing to get what God intended us to receive from Him. It is as if we have an empty cup in our hands, hoping anyone will fill it up. When we're that desperate, it's amazing what we'll take in and consider precious, even though it's scandalous in comparison to the real thing.

Nothing measures up to the pure living water found in Jesus Christ. Only He alone can fill our hearts, minds, and souls with His cleansing truth, refreshing hope, and soul-filling love.

READ

John 7:25-44

RESPOND

God, I believe Jesus extends to me an invitation to come and drink, and by doing so rivers of living water will flow from my heart. Forgive me for the way I go to the people You've put in my life for the kind of fulfillment You designed for me to find in Jesus. Please fill me to the brim with rivers of living water, so more of You may flow forth from my heart. In Jesus' name, amen.

REFLECT

How have you gone from person to person and thing to thing in search of a fill-up instead of going straight to God?

86

Kept and Recorded

You keep track of all my sorrows. You have collected all my tears in your bottle. You have recorded each one in your book.

PSALM 56:8

What do you think it says about the character of God that He promises to keep all our sorrows and tears in a bottle? Oh, my, how many He must have stored up.

Everywhere we turn, we experience the effects of the fall and the reality of suffering. From a battle with cancer to a horrific car accident. From the betrayal of a spouse to the utter demise of a marriage. From a falling out in a friendship to the collapse of a successful company.

The trials and disappointments we face are too numerous to count. They bombard us daily, sometimes moment by moment. But how do we react to them? Do we pitch a fit and stomp our feet? Cry buckets of tears? Crawl into a fetal position? Some of us go quiet. Some of us paint on a smile and pull up our bootstraps pressing on without much said.

Our mere human souls can't handle all the sorrows and tears that come our way, but God can.

The God of the universe, the Creator of this world, promises to store up our tears and record our pain. He sees. He knows. He hears. He responds. God is not absent. He is very much present, taking note of every tear and every sorrow until we meet Him face-to-face.

READ

Psalm 56:8-13

RESPOND

God, I believe You keep track of all my sorrows, for You have collected my tears in a bottle and recorded each one in Your book. Lord, help me see who You really are through this truth—that not one tear shed by me goes unnoticed by You. You care about me and my pain. Help me trust You more and more in times of suffering. In Jesus' name, amen.

REFLECT

How does the truth that God sees your sorrow and holds your tears change what you think of Him, especially as you face times of suffering?

87

Proven Promises

God's way is perfect. All the Lord's promises prove true.
He is a shield for all who look to him for protection.

2 SAMUEL 22:31

Do you sometimes wonder if God's way is really perfect? That His promises are really true? Are you tempted to quit your faith, especially when it seems nothing is going right? I've been there more than a time or two. Like that time I stood at the kitchen sink, tears flowing hard onto the dirty dishes. I could have turned the faucet off and used my own waterworks to get the job done. I was so angry with God, I told Him I was done with Him. How funny, since in telling God I was done, I was actually still talking to Him. The very God I wanted out of my life was the One I was running to in my pain.

I couldn't get my mind around why God let Jeff die. Why did He allow the brain tumor in the first place? Why did He allow remission? Why did He allow Julie to get pregnant only to end up on bed rest for the next six months? And why did He allow the brain tumor to come back, and eventually take his life before his precious baby girl turned one? Why, God? Why?

God never gave me answers. Not that day at the kitchen sink. And not even now, more than a decade later.

Our doubting of God's ways
doesn't ever change His promises.

Even if we can't explain His promises, His ways are still true. Even when we don't know what to believe in a time of grief, He is still on the throne. Even when our faith wavers, He is still a good Father. Even when we don't understand why He gives and takes away, His love is always present in our lives.

God is still there. He is our Strength. He is our Guide. And He is our Protector against the Enemy's effort, even when doubt is the tactic intended to steal us away and send us down what could be the darkest road of our lives. He is still there.

READ

2 Samuel 22:31-37

RESPOND

God, I believe Your ways are perfect, all Your promises prove true, and You are a shield to me when I look toward You for protection. Thank You that Your faithfulness to Your Word and Your promises is not hinged on my faithfulness to You. Thank You for loving me, even when I want to quit and run from You. In Jesus' name, amen.

REFLECT

How has God been faithful to carry you through times of suffering?

88

Tell Them

The dead cannot praise you; they cannot raise their voices in praise. Those who go down to the grave can no longer hope in your faithfulness. Only the living can praise you as I do today. Each generation tells of your faithfulness to the next.

ISAIAH 38:18-19

I'm sure you agree: the dead cannot praise God or declare His faithfulness. But when you read this verse, do you wonder a little about why the obvious is being stated? That's why I find it so helpful to know the backstory when it comes to studying Scripture.

This particular passage describes the lament of King Hezekiah on the brink of his death. These words proclaiming that only the living can praise God were actually spoken by a man about to meet his Maker. How common of mankind! Don't we all find ourselves suddenly full of great revelation when life is being snatched from us? In times like that, we become a tad more intentional about our faith and life on this side of heaven. We recommit to going to church, serving others, being kinder—at first. But often as the crisis passes, we go back to the way we were, taking for granted that every breath is a gift from God.

What if we kept this sense of purpose and passion alive, realizing it's up to us, in the land of the living, to pass on the truth of who God is—in the fire and through the storm, and in the calm and mundane everyday—to the next generation. What would have to change in our everyday lives to keep this mission and legacy-building calling fresh and focused?

When we personally encounter God's faithfulness and forgiveness, healing and holiness, love and redemption, grace and mercy, we can't help but praise Him.

It's up to us to tell the next generation who God is and what He accomplishes—in spite of our mistakes and mishaps! So will we make time to cultivate the kind of intimate relationship with God in which praise would naturally and consistently form on our lips, long before our time comes to meet Him face-to-face?

READ

Isaiah 38:16-20

RESPOND

God, I believe the dead cannot praise You, and those who go down to the grave can no longer hope in Your faithfulness, but only the living can praise You; therefore I am called to tell each generation of Your faithfulness. Forgive me for the times I forsake praising You. Forgive me for not being proactive in telling the next generation about Your faithfulness. Give me eyes to see the opportunities before me to tell of Your faithfulness to all. In the name of Jesus, amen.

REFLECT

How are you responding to the call to tell the next generation about the faithfulness of God?

89

Shine On

Let your light shine everywhere you go, that you may illumine creation, so men and women everywhere may see your good actions, may see creation at its fullest, may see your devotion to Me, and may turn and praise your Father in heaven because of it.

MATTHEW 5:16 THE VOICE

What would happen if you shined the light of Christ everywhere you go? Can you imagine how that might cause those you do life with on a daily basis to praise your Father in heaven?

Living at a boarding school is like being on display all the time. Everything you do, everything you say, every move you make is seen. The one good thing about being watched so closely is that you can't help but feel accountable. Your colleagues watch you interact with your spouse. Your children see you interact with students. Your students watch how you live your life between the classroom bells. They can even figure out which family the faculty kids belong to, simply by picking up on their swagger and hearing the sound of their voices—it was brand identity, so to speak.

I can't help but think that at the heart of this verse from Matthew is the call to understand that we, as Christ followers, also represent a brand. How we live and move, the way we speak and react, our daily actions and devotions, all reveal who we really belong to (John 8:47; 1 Corinthians 3:23).

We are His disciples. His ambassadors. His children. We are "brand" Jesus.

So will we live as children of God, making room in our hearts for His fullness to dwell? Making space in our lives to serve Him wholeheartedly? Making choices that reflect our deep devotion to the One True God? And shining His light for all to see the Light of the World, Jesus Christ, for themselves?

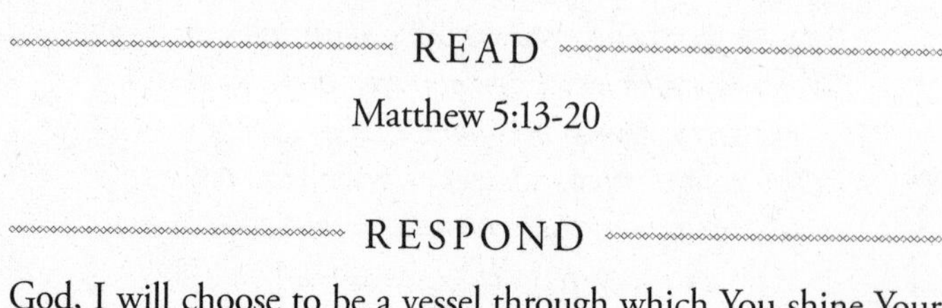

READ

Matthew 5:13-20

RESPOND

God, I will choose to be a vessel through which You shine Your light brightly, so everywhere I go, everyone may see through my actions my devotion to You, and through my testimony would turn to You. Forgive me, God, for the times I've not considered my words and deeds from the perspective of my testimony. Please dwell within me, so Your light may shine through me and people may be drawn to You. In Jesus' name, amen.

REFLECT

How are you representing "brand Jesus" by being a shining light in your actions and devotion to God, and thereby drawing people to want to know Him personally?

90

May God Be with You

Dear brothers and sisters, I close my letter with these last words: Be joyful. Grow to maturity. Encourage each other. Live in harmony and peace. Then the God of love and peace will be with you... May the grace of the Lord Jesus Christ, the love of God, and the fellowship of the Holy Spirit be with you all.

2 CORINTHIANS 13:11,14

When was the last time you received a letter from a friend urging you to embrace the ways of God, the fullness of His presence, and the truth found in the Word? Well, in a way, that's what you've been holding in your hands. It might be called a devotional, but truly, I've written this book in the same way I'd write a letter to my dearest friends. Within these pages, I've shared with you my journey of faith, hoping to pass on to you what has been poured into me—through God Himself, the work of Jesus, the Holy Spirit, and those who have been the hands and feet of Christ to me.

Brooke was one of those people. She showed up in my life shortly after one of my dearest friends moved away. I'd had enough loss for a season, so I wasn't exactly interested in cultivating a new friendship. But Brooke wouldn't take no for an answer as she pushed her way into my life and became a much-needed colaborer in my mentoring ministry. Our friendship went deep fast as we spent much time together each week reading Scripture and discussing how to live in light of biblical values. She encouraged me to slow down, to sit with the Lord and meditate on the truths of God, even if they made me uncomfortable. God used Brooke to nurture my soul and prepare me for the next season of life in a fragile community that needed my leadership. She modeled for me the kind of fellowship God calls us to engage in—the kind we see with Paul and those he served alongside and led to follow Christ. So you could imagine my anger with God when He rerouted her family hundreds of miles away less than 12 months from the day we met. My pouting was less than adultish as I grieved another loss.

> God doesn't waste a second in our lives. He uses even our passing connections in His sanctifying and transforming work.

Eventually the grief over Brooke moving turned into gratitude for the time we had together. As you go forth from this 90-day journey of believing God's Word, I pray you will take what you've received and continue to build upon it as you grow into spiritual maturity. I pray you'll look at life with a new set of lenses, as you believe God's Word as truth and think about who you can share this Good News with.

It is my prayer that you would be a vessel overflowing with hope and joy that comes from God. May you be the example of what it looks like to own your sin and walk in godly sorrow, forgiven and redeemed by the blood of Jesus. May you be the one who suffers for the glory of God, becoming a bright light that points to Jesus Christ. May you become the encourager in your family and community. May you be the peacemaker in your relationships and the grace giver at work and in ministry. May you be a storyteller of God's glorious deeds, conveying to the next generation His faithfulness. And may you always live with unblinded faith, believing that God's Word is the truth!

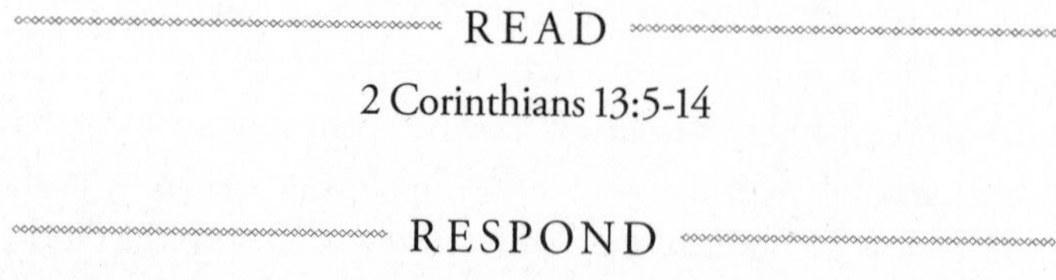

READ

2 Corinthians 13:5-14

RESPOND

God, I receive the challenge to be joyful, grow in maturity, encourage others, and live in harmony and peace so You, the God of love and peace, will be with me and I may experience the grace of Jesus Christ, the fullness of Your love, and the fellowship of the Holy

Spirit, with a purpose of passing it on to others. Please, Lord, give me an ever-growing hunger for Your Word and a constant desire to pursue Your joy, Your peace, Your never-ending love, that I may be a testimony and encourager to those You appoint me to do life with. In Jesus' name, amen.

REFLECT

How is God urging you to not give up, but to press on living for Him and inviting others to say yes to believing His Word as truth?

Head on over to http://www.unblindedfaith.com/purpose/ to download the "On Purpose" resource to help you set short-term and long-term goals for your spiritual growth and legacy-building impact.

Acknowledgments

I am incredibly grateful to my supportive agent, Ruth Samsel of the William K. Jensen Agency, who continually considers how to steward the work and words God has for me in this calling.

I am humbled by the investment of Kathleen Kerr, my editor at Harvest House, who conceived this devotional, bringing into reality a project I prayed about for nearly a year but never spoke a word of to anyone but my husband. Don't you love how God orchestrates the details? LaRae Weikert, I count it a privilege to transcribe these words on your watch. Thank you for your sincere support of this calling. To the rest of the Harvest House team, your effort is remarkable and beautiful.

For my dear friends and beloved mentors at SBS and TVC, you indeed grew me up in the Word and were used by the Holy Spirit to impart such beautiful wisdom and a hunger for truth. For my WLW sisters, Friday Fellowship sisters, "The Squad," and our CCC small group, thanks for praying me through this particular writing journey—I'm grateful for each one of you!

Pastor Burch, the time you took to proof my theology was such a tremendous gift, only outdone by the words of affirmation you sowed into my heart. I am incredibly grateful for your leadership of our church body and your utmost devotion to God as well as the teaching of His Word.

Stephen, thank you for being my out-loud processor and hold-down-the-fort partner. But most of all, thank you for being Christ-with-skin-on to me for the last twenty-five years. Kiddos, this book happened because we're a team. Leah, you sustained us with scrumptious meals and shuttle service. Abby, you kept life in order with your attentiveness to the chores. Luke, your mint-snagging, kiss-on-the-check interruptions were perfectly timed for spurring me on. Kaitlyn, you just might be my greatest cheerleader, always providing the reward of spending time together when I'm "finally" done. I love you, my people, more than all the words I'll ever write in my lifetime.

And most of all, I am exceedingly grateful to God. My life purpose indeed began when I said *yes* to Jesus as my Lord and began to live a life of unblinded faith. Thank You, Father, for breathing life into my soul, my heart, my mind, and my life, when You made me Your chosen, holy, and dearly loved daughter.

About the Author

Elisa Pulliam is the author of *Meet the New You* and founder of the ministry More to Be. She is a certified life coach, mentor, and speaker who is passionate about helping women to experience authentic life change and lasting impact through a fresh encounter with God and His Word for the sake of influencing the next generation. Elisa and her husband, Stephen, savor life together with their four children. Learn more at MoretoBe.com.

Notes

1. *Strong's Lexicon*, s.v. "qadowsh" (Strong's H6918), available on Blue Letter Bible at https://www.blueletterbible.org/lang/lexicon/lexicon.cfm?Strongs=H6918&t=KJV (accessed October 25, 2017).
2. Angela Epstein, "What happens to your body while you're asleep," *Daily Mail,* December 18, 2001, http://www.dailymail.co.uk/health/article-90598/What-happens-body-youre-asleep.html.
3. *Strong's Lexicon*, s.v. "kainos" (Strong's G2537), available on Blue Letter Bible at https://www.blueletterbible.org/lang/lexicon/lexicon.cfm?Strongs=G2537&t=NLT.
4. *Strong's Lexicon*, s.v. "perissos" (Strong's G4053), available on Blue Letter Bible at https://www.blueletterbible.org/lang/lexicon/lexicon.cfm?Strongs=G4053&t=KJV.
5. *Strong's Lexicon*, s.v. "tsar" (Strong's H6862), available on Blue Letter Bible at https://www.blueletterbible.org/lang/lexicon/lexicon.cfm?Strongs=H6862&t=NLT.
6. Source: https://www.blueletterbible.org/lang/lexicon/lexicon.cfm?Strongs=G89&t=NLT.
7. Source: https://www.blueletterbible.org/lang/lexicon/lexicon.cfm?Strongs=G4336&t=NLT.
8. Source: https://en.wikipedia.org/wiki/Dayenu and https://jewsforjesus.org/for-congregations/christ-in-the-passover/christ-in-the-passover-music-and-lyrics/.
9. *Strong's Lexicon*, s.v. "agape" (Strong's G26), available on Blue Letter Bible at https://www.blueletterbible.org/lang/lexicon/lexicon.cfm?Strongs=G26&t=NLT.
10. Trent C. Butler, *Holman Bible Dictionary* (Nashville, Holman Bible Publishers, 1991), 897.